a sacrificial poet

john shirk

Dedicated to the amazing spoken word artists of Chicago who are helping me become an echo of the Sacrificial Poet.

contents

chapter 1 waiting for isaac 19

chapter 2 coming out of the closet 25

chapter 3 what Is christianity? 29

chapter 4 if someday we stand at the gates of heaven 31

chapter 5 the Sacrificial Poet arrives 35

chapter 6 far from God 39

chapter 7 too broken for amazing grace 41

chapter 8 the greatest commandment 45

chapter 9 the least likely person 47

chapter 10 the Sacrificial Poet exposes the deep dark secret . . 51

chapter 11 a least likely sacrificial poet 53

chapter 12 their God who hates me 57

chapter 13 the Sacrificial Poet weeps 61

chapter 14 am i a hater? 63

chapter 15 the lost words of the Sacrificial Poet 65

chapter 16 soft on sin? 67

chapter 17 who wants to be a conversion project? part 1 71

chapter 18 evil evangelism 73

chapter 19 who wants to be a conversion project? part 2 75

chapter 20 who wants to be a christian? 77

chapter 21 conversions or conversations? 79

chapter 22 between two worlds 81

chapter 23 overreacting 83

chapter 24 a church that's irrelevant 87

chapter 25 a church that's too relevant 89

chapter 26 two kinds of people 91

chapter 27 broken 93

chapter 28 a tale of two families 95

chapter 29 the Artist 97

chapter 30 real church 99

chapter 31 choose your chapter 103

chapter 32 for my christian family 105

chapter 32 for my poetry family 109

chapter 33 waiting for adam 111

epilogue   why i believe 115

the prequel   The Sacrificial Poet 117

acknowledgements

I never thought I would write a book. I have the attention span of a spoken word poet. Anything longer than three minutes and I begin to get overwhelmed. For that reason, this book would never have come about had it not been for the help and influence of so many people.

There are those who have lived this journey with me—my wife Amy, my daughters Elizabeth, Esther, Emma, and Elena, and my parents Glen and Lois. Without them, this crazy adventure could not have taken place.

The churches and individuals who have prayed and financially supported my ministry are also important. There are too many to name but the folks at Community Grace Brethren Church in Warsaw Indiana and Ripon Grace in Ripon California deserve special mention. Along with them I would include Kurt Miller, Ron Boehm, and Clive Craigen from my days with Grace Brethren North American Missions.

But that is only half of the story. This book would have never been written if the amazing spoken word poets from Chicago had not welcomed me into their world. There are way too many to include all of their names here but the folks from Mental Graffiti, Weeds, In One Ear, and PolyRhythmic deserve special thanks.

Even with all that, this book might not have happened. I probably owe at least a passing acknowledgement to Phil Long who convinced me to write it—three minutes at a time. He visited Chicago and listened to many of these stories before insisting that others should hear them too. It was in the car on the way home from dropping him off at the airport that I realized I had no choice but to write.

Others who were key include J.D. Woods who did the cover art, Miriam Pacheco and Gladys Deloe who helped with editing, Terry White and Evan Dunn who helped me begin to understand publishing, and Kathy Young who took care of typesetting and layout.

Others I wish to thank for investing in my life and helping to mold my thinking include Gary McCaman, Galen Wiley, Kynshasa and Ellen Ward, Bob and Julie Combs, and John Fischer. To all the rest of you who know you played a part but are not mentioned, please know that the gratefulness in my heart is for you as well.

Most of all, this sacrificial poet wishes to thank the Sacrificial Poet whose poem of redemption echoes throughout history showing the way home.

forward

My entanglement with John Shirk began a couple of years before we met so I'm not quite sure where to begin our story. There are times in one's life that only make sense if the possibility of forces let's say, "beyond nature," are allowed to have played a role. My relationship with John is just such a case. Let me explain.

In spring of 2011, shortly after we met, John sent me an email in which he suggested I sit down before reading on because he had a surprise for me. Details he shared in that email forced me to consider that my own choices over the previous two years may have somehow been manipulated or influenced in ways I cannot explain. It all now seems related to his prayerful intervention that began well before we met. I know it sounds confusing so I'll circle back and pick up some pieces.

In the fall of 2008 I walked into the Seattle Poetry Slam for the first time. It was October and I had driven to Seattle determined to compete in my very first poetry competition. I had written an original poem and performed it before various audiences for several months prior to that night and had just learned that it was considered a slam poem. I decided to drive three hours north to Seattle for a chance to perform. As it turned out, I needed three poems to compete in the slam competition and only had one. They took pity and allowed me to sign up for the open mic instead. One vivid memory I have of the evening was the discomfort I experienced listening to the raw, uncensored, and quite vulgar honesty that sometimes is a part of slam poetry. Conversely, I also remember a warm and welcoming audience responding appreciatively to my overtly "Christian" poem.

The first person to speak to me after the competition that night was a very encouraging young woman who said she enjoyed my poem and that I should try to connect with her poet friend from Chicago some day since he wrote similar faith-related poetry. On the way home that night I concluded that I belonged in this scene and resolved to find a way to connect with and join the creative conversation.

Long after that first poetry slam experience, I heard about John. A friend had sent me a blog post about a poet in Chicago who frequented the open mics and poetry slams and who also happened to be a Christian. John and I connected with the help of the blogger and we began to exchange email. We had a lot to talk about. We shared our interest and connections in the slam world. He was a regular in the scene for over eight years at the time with many poet friends and lots of experience. It was clear that he really loved the poets he had met along the way. I was an airline pilot just recently hitting slams all over the country while on layovers and loving the human drama and artistic brilliance of the whole scene, but with very few poet friends yet. We shared a common faith, a common interest in spoken word poetry, and a deep appreciation for the clever and artistic wordsmiths who inhabited the performance poetry community. We had a passion to engage them in faith conversations within the open and honest anything-goes slam poetry world.

A few weeks after meeting John in 2011, I received his email advising me to take a seat before reading on. In that email, and in subsequent conversations he revealed that he might be the very reason I got into poetry slams in the first place back in 2008. John had looked at the calendar. In September of 2008 he met a young lady poet who was touring in Chicago. He had had the pleasure of having her in his home for lunch and a remarkable conversation about faith. When she flew back to the West Coast, he began praying with some friends that God would send another Christian into her life to join the conversation. A month later, I drove three hours to the Seattle poetry slam where I would meet her and decide to join the poetic dialogue and spend my life engaging the incredible world of spoken word poetry.

Of course, I do understand that it could all be coincidence. But to make this even more convoluted, I should remind you that I began to write poetry thirty years before he prayed, finished my first slam poem six months before he prayed, and attended that poetry slam in Seattle where I met his poet friend who mentioned his name without even knowing that he had prayed. All this random connectedness might be easy for me to dismiss as mere accident but dismissing it would not erase the chills that struck my spine when the very question I had entertained for over a year—asking why I felt so drawn to this spoken word poetry thing at all—was decisively answered!

It was only after John told me about his friend and his prayers for her that I suddenly realized, when she approached me that first night in Seattle, she was talking about him. John was her poet friend from Chicago who wrote about faith! What?! You can't make this stuff up; John and I met and became friends before he realized I was the unlikely answer to his prayers and before I realized that he was the guy I was told about at my first poetry slam by the very woman he was praying for. So we just happened to become friends? Fine, you can say it's a coincidence. It still gives me the willies.

This book is John's story about seeing God at work in the world of spoken word poetry. It's easy to see that He is at work. I've seen, first hand, the special kind of humility and sincere love for others God has given John in the midst of it all. During a visit to Chicago near Thanksgiving in 2011, John took me to several of his favorite open mic venues—The Green Mill, Mental Graffiti, and Weeds—to introduce me to his poetry friends. I witnessed how he cared for them and how they loved, trusted, and appreciated him in return. I also noticed how he was on high alert for any gross buffoonery that I might suddenly perpetrate among his poet friends.

I left Chicago convinced that any Christian who thinks they need to share their faith in the spoken word poetry slam world ought to spend some time with John Shirk and learn from him. There are plenty of wannabe poet-evangelists who have no love, respect, or understanding of the poets they target with their drive-by testimonies and insensitive demands to profess a cliché Christian faith as they herald a myopic version of the good news while entirely detached from their audience. Given the ubiquitous and sometimes well-deserved suspicion towards self-righteous Christians, John's life demonstrates that it's better to pay the welcome price of sincere friendship and earn the right to have a meaningful conversation.

I'm fairly certain that John's story will both bother and entice you. It's open and honest. It's like an open mic performance. There are very few public places left in our culture where human beings can be so creative and vulnerable in such a supportive and encouraging environment as a slam poetry open mic. It's a privilege to be accepted in this community. It's an honor to have the opportunity to share and learn and grow with so many artists coming from such different perspectives. It's no surprise that God would choose such a place to refine His poets and their art.

Before a poetry slam begins, the host will often declare that the competition cannot proceed until blood has been spilled upon the stage. And with that, they invite a "sacrificial poet" to the stage to help calibrate the newly selected audience-judges for the night. John has been around the open mic often enough to know that, if we want to follow Jesus into the spoken word poetry scene, we must become sacrificial poets. Better to humbly follow the way of the Sacrificial Poet we claim as Lord than pay over-eager lip service with empty words and empty hearts. John knows how to follow. I hope you'll read this book and learn from him. I hope you read this book and catch a glimpse of God at work. Every time I listen to John I discover another way that God has shaped him through the experience of becoming a sacrificial poet. And then I wonder what this "fairytale-God-poet" who is clearly "writing souls into eternity with dust" will do next.

For more information on the *Sacrificial Poet Project* or to support sacrificial poets who are seeking to engage both the slam community and the church in a conversation about the Sacrificial Poet, Jesus Christ, check out http://sacrificialpoetproject.org

Phil Long (aka *Liar Lunatic*) is a spoken word artist, author, playwright, actor, creator of the Jesus Poetry Slam, and founder/director of the nonprofit Sacrificial Poet Project.

the judges scores

The sacrificial poet plays an important role at poetry slams. Judges are selected randomly from the audience and often have little or no experience. The first poet often receives the lowest scores. Then as the judges feel pressured by the audience the scores tend creep up giving later poets an advantage. As a result, no one wants to go first.

This is the role of a sacrificial poet. While not a part of the competition, they go first pouring their heart and soul into a poem to be scored by the judges. They have no hope of winning the slam. Instead they are rewarded with the knowledge their voice was heard, and the satisfaction of knowing they helped make the slam fairer for the poets that would follow.

As I was thinking about this tradition, I realized "a sacrificial poet" must also face the judges. So I have recruited some of my friends from the spoken word community to judge "a sacrificial poet" on a scale of 1 to 10.

Dan Sullivan

I'm giving John's book an 8.9 and I'll tell you, it's not because I don't think it's a wonderful book. It certainly is. I'm giving it an 8.9 because it shows us that our journey is never complete. At the point we think we have things figured out and have our perfect score, God, or life, or our communities, our neighbors, our families, they tend to hold up the mirror and show us how much more room for growth we have. In *a sacrificial poet,* John takes us on an imperfect journey toward growth, light and learning. There are lessons we can all learn from within the pages of this book, because we all have hearts that need to be torn open, deconstructed and rebuilt.

Dan "Sully" Sullivan has appeared on Russell Simmons Presents Def Poetry on HBO and National Public Radio. He is the Chicago Mental Graffiti 2003, 04, & 05 Poetry Slam Champion and the recipient of The 2003 Gwendolyn Brooks Open Mic Poetry Award. Sully is a member of The Speak'Easy Ensemble directed by Marc "So What!" Smith, is the Co-Founder of the Oak Park River Forest High School Spoken Word Club and The Urban Sandbox, an all-ages community open mic. Sully has been published in several magazines & anthologies including *The*

Columbia Poetry Review, Learn Then Burn: A Modern Poetry Anthology for the Classroom, & Poems From The Big Muddy: The 2004 National Poetry Slam Anthology.

J.W. Basilo

John Shirk's memoir speaks from a place of true reflection and exploration that one doesn't see to often in books that try to tackle faith. As both a poet and disavowed Catholic, I really enjoyed reading about John's journey and the discoveries that lie therein. If anyone was going to bring me to Jesus, it would be John Shirk—But don't get any ideas. I'd give this sacrificial poet an 8.7.

J.W. Basilo is a National and World Poetry Slam finalist, a PushCart Prize Nominee, one half of Poetry/Comedy duo Beard Fight (with Dan Sully), and an Artist in Residence at Real Talk Avenue. His work has appeared on NPR, CBS, WGN, in the Chicago Tribune, numerous literary journals, and in hundreds of theaters, dive bars, prisons, schools and comedy clubs across the world. Basilo is the Executive Director of Chicago Slam Works, a non-profit dedicated to producing the finest shows in Chicago's live literature community. You can catch him Sunday evenings at the Green Mill where he co-hosts the world-famous Uptown Poetry Slam.

Emelia Zuckerman

I've never judged a poetry slam, so I'm going to go ahead and give it a 9.5. That's pretty good right? John's writing is evocative, without being overly sentimental, as always. I definitely think John should keep writing, and that you, dear reader keep reading.

Emelia Zuckerman is a sometimes poet and all the time Artistic Director of Chicago based Forget Me Not Theatre Company.

Gregorio Gomez

Trouble had been brewing in the bowels of the 2nd city's poetry community and its venues. . .poets or patrons, alike, would not escape unscathed from the rage of the tempest to arrive. . .with the poetry world in disarray, John Shirk and family (his wife; a notorious preacher extraordinaire, and daughters; those smooth swift talking bible agents disguised as little girls) descend upon the city of winds. . .

A literally literary chitown fire looms. . .a l-o-n-g, s-lo-w simmering love affair boils. . .a dastardly plot twinkles and twirls and swirls like a venomous python slithering on the dark dingy parquet of the open mic readings. . .and the hill street blues of this city beneath its skyscrapers. . .

There is no evading the onrushing that threatens the very fiber of the poets and their lot. . .so John Shirk and his crack team of agents. . .plunge feet first with cudgel in hand, into the eye of the needle, which is the middle. . .that represents the center. . .Shall I dare say *"the very core of the hurricane"*. . .

I rate it a horrible 9. . .read at your own peril. . .

Gregorio Gomez is the MC of Chicago's most infamous and longest running underground poetry venue at "WEEDS". Gregorio, who emigrated from Veracruz, Mexico has been a major influence in the development of the spoken word and many venues of Chicago's poetry community for two decades.

M.C. Rydel

In "a sacrificial poet," John Shirk describes Chicago's spoken word poetry scene from the point of view of a Christian missionary evangelizing the Bohemians. Shirk's memoir uncovers the spirituality of his congregation, his own poetic voice, and a new path to a real Jesus, revealing his voice in the rhyme.

Grade: A+ So good- No slam score needed!

M.C. Rydel reads his poetry at the In One Ear Open Mic and teaches writing and literature at Loyola. Not a slam poet, M.C's more comfortable in the classroom and obviously grades on a curve.

Gregory Pickett

8.9

I didn't know what to expect when I opened the book to the first page. Even though I'm a spoken word artist/performance poet I loathe reading, but this was an enjoyable read. The idea of God being the Sacrificial Poet is probably one of the most poetic things I've ever heard. As a poet and Christian (the Christian part is relatively new for me) I found myself learning more about my faith than about the poetry scene after reading. If there were more of a balance between the poetry scene and faith, I would have scored a 9. (yeah, I'm THAT guy who gives Big Poppa Shirk less than 9). But that's real. And John has been nothing but "real" with me the moment we met. Like everything in this book is about as "real" as it gets. In slam, we have a mantra that's along the lines of "leaving it all on the stage". John Shirk certainly "left it all on the page" here.

Gregory Pickett believes that poetry can foster life's evolutions, transitions, and changes. Using poetry, he has transformed from a shaman, into a wolf, into a lion. Pickett has performed everywhere from convention centers in Boston to street corners in Chicago. No matter the place, the audience never forgets his roar. In 2009 he won the 3rd Annual Rootabaga Poetry Slam, in Galesburg, IL, received 2nd Place in the 3rd annual Online Virtual Poetry Slam hosted by Citizens for Global Solutions, and placed 3rd in the Mental Graffiti Grand Slam, earning him a place on the Mental Graffiti Slam Team, which competed at the 2009 National Poetry Slam. In 2013 He was the Lethal Poetry Grand Slam Champion, competed at the National Poetry Slam in Boston and was a Gwendolyn Brooks Open Mic Awards Semi-Finalist.

Tim Cook

In *a sacrificial poet*, John Shirk recounts lucidly and with philosophical depth how he chose his own adventure, a missionary quest into Chicago's spoken word poetry community. But rather than either converting presumably faithless slam poets or having his faith compromised, his perspective changed about urban poets, Evangelical Christians, and himself, leading ultimately to a greater acceptance of both the brokenness and redeemability of us all.

Score: 13.11--By candidly and unflinchingly examining his inner self, John is putting away childish things.

Timothy Cook, a Chicago native, graduated from Loyola University with a BA in philosophy and from the MFA Program for Writers at Warren Wilson College. He represented the Green Mill at the National Poetry Slam, was Slammaster and host of Poetry Slam Asheville, and currently co-hosts the Mental Graffiti Poetry Slam. He is a recipient of a grant from the Mookie Jam Foundation, which supports artists living with multiple sclerosis.

Amy David

9.1! "a sacrificial poet" is a fascinating look at spirituality, humility, and most importantly, community. Shirk's memoir captures an essential piece of history for the Chicago poetry scene, and is a must-read for anyone interested in how we all learn to love one another through art.

Amy David has represented Chicago four times at the National Poetry Slam, and her work has appeared in journals including Word Riot, Foundling Review, and Super Arrow. She co-organized the Mental

Graffiti poetry slam for two years, and was a founding board member of Chicago Slam Works.

Adrienne Nadeau

At John Shirk's first poetry show, he asked himself "What if I was called to be a sacrificial poet? Someone willing to bare his soul, be judged by the crowd, and take whatever came next." I've always felt a spiritual connection at open mics, from the sincerity of the confessions, the camaraderie of the community or the rituals of the show, it's almost impossible not to be moved. John's journey both as a poet and a Christian is engaging and honest and paints a nostalgic portrait of Chicago poetry and the shows that started it all. 8.7

Adrienne Nadeau moved to Chicago four years ago but happily calls the Windy City home. In her short time in the Midwest, Adrienne has represented Mental Graffiti (2011) and Lethal Poetry (2013) at the National Poetry Slam and currently runs the Words That Kill open mic night with the rest of the Lethal Poetry collective. Additionally, she has represented Chicago at the Great Plains Poetry Pile Up, the Ekphrastic Slam, and Southern Fried Regional Slam. In 2013, she joined the associate board of Chicago Slam Works as the Volunteer Coordinator and is humbly helping them achieve their mission of igniting the city with live literary events.

Chelsea Fiddyment

"I wondered what a Christ-following performance poet would look (and sound) like," John asks, and in this book, he gives us one possible execution. I'm not a Chicagoan, I'm not a Christian, and I'm sure as hell not a slam poet. But I believe in the power of text to change us, to help us discover and understand ourselves, which in turn helps us to better understand others around us. John's text is as much as about a belief in text, change, and Scripture as it is about showing us his continued journey of personal and spiritual change. It is about poetry and poets and The Poet. It is about growth, and is a call to grow in ourselves; it is as much about cultivating a belief in words as in The Word.

I wondered, too, what the book of a Christ-following performance poet would look like—and in John's case, it is a careful curation of powerful poems (and given what this book is about, I include Scripture under the heading of poetry) and compelling anecdotes, masterfully arranged into a cohesive, compelling narrative. If you never hear John Shirk perform, *a sacrificial poet* is a more than acceptable substitute. The words contained within are rich with his good-natured humor, his stylistic cadence, his conceptual pacing, his humility. His devotion to love rings as clearly here as it does in his every reading aloud.

Is this book preachy? Perhaps, if by "preachy" we mean it comes with a message. But John's voice and skilled arrangement of the text keep us in our seats, listening—not because we feel forced, but because he writes and edits with the eyes, ears, and heart of someone who has built his life on listening, who believes, as with the reading of text, that listening deepens our knowledge of our existence, of this life, of ourselves. Some time ago, John "[came] to the conclusion that sometimes pop music and slam poetry get things right." *a sacrificial poet* gets it right, and gets a solid 7.9 from me.

Chelsea Fiddyment is a word and language artist based in Chicago, IL. She works in short fiction, book forms and construction, and visual and hybrid texts. She is a classically-trained vocalist who has been, in no particular order, a barista, an IHOP host, a writing tutor, a jazz singer, and a floral delivery person. She holds a B.A. in English and Creative Writing from the University of Illinois and an M.F.A. in Writing from the School of the Art Institute of Chicago.

chapter 1

waiting for isaac

The evening started with the open mic. It wasn't long before I discovered this was not the poetry of Shakespeare or Frost, and it definitely wasn't the poetry of Great Grandpa Cover or Grandma Miller. There were no rules regarding meter or form, and most of it didn't rhyme. But beyond the style, the issues it raised and the language it used were very different. It was liberally sprinkled with obscenity, occasionally crossing into R- or even X-rated themes, along with political rants about what was wrong with America and our President.

I hadn't planned an evening like this. But as I walked down Milwaukee Avenue I happened across a couple of young men outside a bar. It appeared they were just standing around, so I struck up a conversation. They were waiting to go into "Mental Graffiti" an open mic and poetry slam. I thought I knew what poetry was, but really I had no idea. My thoughts of poetry involved the long dead poets I was forced to learn about in school, as well as the binders of poetry passed down from my grandparents. I couldn't imagine young people and poetry together unless it was forced on them as part of a boring literature class. But the young men I met explained that poetry slams were cool (actually the word was probably "dope" or "fresh"). They invited me to come check it out. It didn't sound like it would compromise my faith, and I was trying to meet people, so I decided to attend. I figured I could try just about anything once, and if things went bad I could always get up and leave.

After the open mic, the slam started. A poetry slam is a competition invented by Marc Smith in Chicago in the 1980s. Marc was a construction worker who wanted to get his buddies to listen to poetry, and decided to make it a competition. The whole thing was really just an excuse to make poetry more interesting and attract an audience.

The young men I met on the street were competing. In the second round, one of them read a poem that would change my life. It was called Waiting for Isaac.

Waiting for Isaac[1]
By Eitan Kadosh

I was desperate
I was dry like the Kalahari
Barren like Sarah
Waiting for Isaac
For the birth of a word
that seemed
just out of reach

So I looked to books
I thought

I could slum it like Bukowski
Live it large like Elliot
Drink it up like Kerouac
Die like Keats—rosy and tubercular
Die like Plath—rosy hughesed asphyxiated
Smoke it like Ginsberg
Bomb like Corso
all that (yeah!)
only more so

I realized quickly what was wrong

I was too sheltered
I was too comfortable
Too warm and dry
A happy pea ensconced in my posh pod
My life was too normal
I needed to take action
I needed to f--- s--- up

So I slept with your sister
So you broke up with me
So I didn't go to work
So I got fired

---

[1] Copyright Eitan Kadosh, used by permission. This version of "Waiting for Isaac" was slightly edited to remove profanity as well as a couple of lines that some readers may find offensive. For an unedited version, see Eitan's chapbook, "Singles." Those interested in Eitan's poetry can reach him at eitankadosh@outlook.com.

So I couldn't pay the rent
So I got evicted
So I couldn't really study
So I failed out of school
So I didn't pay attention
and my dealer sold me a bag of $60 catnip

So I took up Mountain Dew sports
like skydiving and mountain biking
and I broke my collarbone
but it wasn't enough

So I ripped the tag off my mattress
I blow-dried my hair in the bathtub
I slept with your sister again and got crabs
but it wasn't enough

I slept on the sidewalk
it wasn't enough
I slept in the gutter
it wasn't enough

I slept in the gutter on street sweeping days
I ate nothing but Denny's
I burned all my CDs
except for Morissey
. . .

. . .
but it wasn't enough

I started smoking
it wasn't enough
I drank till my liver froze up like an old car
it wasn't enough
I snorted speed was too jittery to hold a pen
shot smack was too content to care
smoked crack in People's Park and was arrested

And it wasn't enough

So I polluted the air
I littered the streets

I bought a sport utility vehicle
I sold vitally important national security documents to
   indiscriminate nations
I melted the polar ice caps
and flooded coastal cities around the world
caused climate change mass starvation
pestilence ran rampant

My life became a living hell
as I made the whole g--d--- world suck
but it wasn't enough

Because I am still waiting for Isaac
because I am still waiting for laughter
for a progeny
that will live on
when I don't

I am still waiting for Isaac
for a re-birth of wonder
and for the intervening hand of a god
I never believed in the first place
to make it happen

I was glad we were in a dimly lit bar, because when he finished I had to fight back tears. I had prayed that God would send me to spiritually sensitive people and here in front of me was a young man waiting "for the intervening hand of a god I never believed in".

Was I not in Chicago as part of the body of Christ? I had sung songs about being His hands and feet. It was obvious to me that my attendance that night was no accident.

Was I not an ambassador sent by Him to intervene in the lives of people? I wanted to grab the young man and tell him about the God who had already intervened, the God who fulfilled His promise to Abraham and Sarah when Isaac was born, the God who fulfilled His promise to Adam and Eve when Christ, the Word made flesh, was born. I wanted to bring him laughter, to watch in wonder as he underwent re-birth.

God had sent me to be His witness. Paul wrote in Galatians that followers of Christ are like Isaac, children of the promise. It was my job to share that promise with the people God was bringing together each Monday night. But how could I do that? To use missionary terminology they seemed like "hard soil". Their dislike for Christianity seemed obvious. I didn't know how God was going to use me to be His witness.

This seemed so raw and so real. But this slam poetry scene was not my world and entering it might cost me. Maybe dearly. I could imagine being a missionary and learning more about poetry but what if I was called to be a sacrificial poet? Someone willing to bare his soul, be judged by the crowd, and take whatever came next. I didn't feel prepared but I felt I had no choice. God had just spoken to me through the words of a slam poet in Chicago. I was in.

Christians who read the previous paragraphs can probably relate. We are tempted to think this way. We are here to fix the world around us. We are here to convert the lost and make disciples. To non-Christians this probably sounds arrogant, maybe even offensive. This book is about how I learned they are right. It's about my journey to discover how arrogant and offensive I was (even if I hid it well). It's about the lessons I have learned through ten years of involvement in Chicago's spoken word community. How I came to Chicago to transform the city, and found God using the city to transform me. I came with the goal of turning the people I met into followers of Jesus, only to find God was using them to teach me what it really means to follow Christ.

chapter 2

coming out of the closet

When Eitan finished his poem, I had my mission and I knew where I belonged. I felt God wanted to intervene in the Chicago poetry scene. I had a God-sized dream of a church of poets using their creative talents in service of the Almighty Creator, the Sacrificial Poet who had written Himself into His masterpiece. But I hadn't the foggiest notion of what that would look like or how to make it happen.

One beauty of an open mic is anyone can sign up and perform anything. I thought about the options open to me. I could have come back the following week with a gospel presentation disguised as a poem. But I had no confidence this would be effective. The atmosphere seemed hostile to Christians and Christianity. This hostility was driven home at an open mic some time later when an out-of-town poet prefaced his performance with a question "Do you want to hear an angry poem about America or a song about God?" It was during the George W. Bush presidency and angry poems about America were fairly commonplace, so the crowd wanted a song about God.

The poet seemed pleased, and asked if there were any Christians present. I had not yet publicly discussed my faith in this crowd but I nervously raised my hand, hoping not to be too obvious. I saw one other hand go up, and that person was laughing as if it were a joke. The poet on stage seemed pleased, and commented that he always liked to offend someone when he read. Then he began to sing, "Jesus Loves Me." At first he sang it all the way through with all the tenderness of a father putting his child to bed. The second time around, however, he had rewritten it using the words of a hateful, bigoted, fundamentalist who believed that Jesus loves me but hates you and is sending you to hell because you are a sinner. He couldn't have painted Christians in a worse light. The crowd loved it. And I wondered if there was really room for a follower of Jesus at the open mic.

However, in spite of their apparent disdain for evangelical Christianity and the church, they were a very tolerant group that valued diversity. There were poets from several different races and ethnic groups. There were poets from various religious backgrounds and sexual orientations.

The one thing that seemed to be missing was a follower of Christ. I wondered what a Christ-following performance poet would look (and sound) like. I realized there were two ways I could find out. Turn a poet into a Jesus follower, or turn a Jesus follower into a poet. Only one of those options was under my control. I couldn't change them, but I could change me. If I could become a poet, Mental Graffiti would have a "token Christian."

So my education and transformation began, as I sought to learn the language and customs of the people around me. And like so many missionaries before me, I was dependant on the "natives" to teach me. I attended every Monday night and asked endless questions about writing poetry. I tried to get as much coaching as I could.

Maria was one of the most respected poets on the scene. The matriarch, she was known as "Mama." As I struggled to understand the culture around me she helped me "find my voice," teaching me not to mimic what I heard on the mic but be true to who I was. She helped me understand that poetry, like all art, springs from the soul of the artist. I had to write from my life and experience.

There were other helpful conversations. I remember a visiting poet from Ohio whose advice was to read "classic cats, like William Shakespeare." At the time I still couldn't see the common ground between such classics and what I was hearing each week, but that was due to my ignorance of poetry, not faulty advice on his part. Another poet suggested I spend an hour or two staring at a parking meter, making note of every detail, meditating on what I saw, and writing whatever came to mind.

Some of the most helpful advice came from John, an older poet known as JDub. I remember asking him what made a poem a poem. If it doesn't rhyme or follow any rules, how do you know when it's a poem? JDub explained that anything could be a poem. In fact a poem is a poem if you call it a poem. He told me of a poem he had written called "A Letter to Krystal." It was just like any other letter you might write except he had broken the lines down. This made it look like a poem, and he called it a poem, so it was a poem. I figured if there were no rules I couldn't break them, and I started writing poetry.

I quickly learned that although "a poem is a poem if you call it a poem," that doesn't make it a good poem. My earliest attempts at poetry left a lot to be desired. Some of it was silly, like my poem about why I couldn't write poetry. I decided if you write about why you can't write, and the writing is bad, that just proves your point. I knew that if I wrote about typical poetry topics like politics I was guaranteed to lose. I would be competing against the best poets on the scene. I could never be that good. So I wrote a love poem to my three small daughters. No one else was doing that, so at least I was original. I also wrote a poem about a man we had met doing ministry to the homeless under an overpass. It referenced the teaching of Christ, but did so in a very subtle way, mostly addressing the problem of poverty and homelessness.

As I was learning about poetry, I was also learning about the poetry scene. The more I got to know the poets at Mental Graffiti, the more I grew to love and respect them. They didn't judge me for being different, and they were very supportive of my feeble attempts at poetry. I also began to see past the profanity and obscenity that seemed so shocking at first. Beneath the raw exterior I found an honest transparency that is rare in the world today. They told stories of their pain and struggle to live in a messed up broken world. They spoke out against injustice. While one might question whether their solutions to the problems of this world were the correct ones, the problems they were seeking to address were real.

But even as I fell in love with the poetry scene, there was always a nagging question in the back of my mind. "Will they still tolerate me when they find out I'm a Christian?"

The relationships grew, and soon I became convinced it was time to write more of my faith into poetry. I set a date when I planned to "come out of the closet" and reveal that I was a Christian, and began writing a poem, which would proclaim my faith in Christ.

When the poem was written, I shared it with one of my friends from Wicker Park. Nicole was the first contact I had made in Chicago. I met her while visiting Chicago before we moved, then reconnected at a coffee shop after we had settled in the city. She was a lesbian who had studied theology at Brigham Young University. She was very open to discussing faith. I told her I was going to "come out of the closet" as a Christian at Mental Graffiti and showed her the poem. She liked it, but she couldn't believe I was planning to read it at an open mic. She said she would show up and clap for me even if no one else did. She also commented about "coming out of the closet."

> In this neighborhood if you come out of the closet and say you are gay, no one will bat an eyelash. You will probably even gain respect in many people's eyes. But if you "come out" and say you are a Christian—now

that might turn some heads. You might face opposition
or rejection. You can probably understand how we feel.

The day to read my poem came. As it happened I unknowingly picked
a week when slam poets from all over the country were in Chicago for
meetings. When I arrived at the Funky Buddha Lounge for Mental Graffiti, the bar was full of people I had never met. This only increased my
anxiety. I had invested months building relationships with the regulars,
but the audience was full of people I had no relationship with at all.
But I had told Nicole I was going to "Come out" and she was there to
support me, so I determined I couldn't chicken out. When I was called
up to the mic, I introduced my poem this way.

> *This poem's a little unusual. It's my criticism of Chris-*
> *tianity. That in itself is not unusual, I've heard several*
> *people criticize Christianity on the mic. This poem is*
> *unusual because I am a Christian. It's criticism from*
> *the inside.*

Then I read the poem.

chapter 3

what is christianity?

Christianity is the slaughter of Muslims
  and the burning of witches at the stake

It is Catholics killing Protestants
  and Protestants killing Catholics

It is Columbus plundering
  and pillaging North America

It is slave ships full of "human property"
  and slave masters selling their own progeny

It is Priests abusing children,
  and Bishops covering it up

It is ornate cathedrals casting uncaring shadows
  on the hungry, sick, and impoverished

It is Televangelists in bed with hookers

It is Prolife murderers

It is Hatred
Racism
Sexism
Homophobia
and Intolerance

It is me
And I'm ashamed

It is me
And I'm sorry

How did this happen?

Christianity began with Christ

The Christ who said
  "Do unto others as you would have them do unto you"
  "Do not judge or you will be judged"

> *"Love your enemies"*
> *"Turn the other cheek"*
>
> *The Christ who*
> > *". . .did not come to be served, but to serve,*
> > *and to give his life as a ransom for many"*
>
> *The Christ who said*
> > *"Follow Me"*
>
> *How did his followers get so far from their leader?*
> *I don't know*
> *but I'm sorry*
>
> *Maybe it is time to abandon Christianity,*
> > *and follow Christ*
>
> *As it is*
> *People hate Christianity*
> *I understand*
> *I'm sorry*

I returned to my seat scared to death of how the audience might respond. Then Anacron, the DJ and co-host got up to introduce the next poet and said,

> *That's why I love John's poetry. He doesn't try to sound like everyone else or write what he thinks you want to hear. He just writes what he thinks.*

That was the kindest gift Anacron could have possibly given me. It was his way of saying to all the visiting poets who may not have known how to respond to this unusual poem, "I know it's not what you are used to, but this guy is one of us. He's okay."

Mental Graffiti had its "token Christian."

chapter 4

if some day we stand at the gates of heaven

I continued to work on my writing, and my cultural lessons continued to expand to areas such as fashion. One night I had said something in jest to Sully over the mic. It was all in fun but when he got even with me by mocking my tucked in shirt I realized I was committing a fashion faux pas. My shirts have remained untucked at open mics ever since.

Now a regular at Mental Graffiti, I also began attending other open mics. The more I got involved, the more I realized how wrong my initial impressions had been. The fears I had about how they would react when they found out I was a Christian were unfounded. They really were tolerant of Christianity, and open to discussing spiritual things. Many were asking questions, unsatisfied with what they had been taught growing up. They loved being part of an honest dialogue and wanted to talk. They just weren't sure they wanted to talk to Christians, because of the reputations we have for talking without listening, preaching judgment and condemnation, and hypocrisy. They wanted a conversation, not a lecture, a sermon or a verdict.

As I learned how to listen and be a friend, the conversations multiplied. I remember one night staying up until 1:30 in the morning discussing spiritual things with Jeff after an open mic in the suburbs. He told me he knew I was praying for him; since God had been at work in his life and I was the only person he knew who might be behind it. Another friend shared his search to find meaning and morality with or without God. He had grown up in a church, and spoke of his loss of faith, and his envy of those who have faith, since their lives often displayed a meaning and purpose that he lacked.

When "The Passion of the Christ" came out, everyone seemed to get passionate. It was just the kind of movie I think my friends might have enjoyed, until churches everywhere made it clear that they were going to use it to proselytize. To my friends, this took it out of the realm of cinema, and into the realm of propaganda. But even though they were not fans of the movie, everyone was talking about it, so I wrote a poem about Jesus to read at the open mic. As I was waiting my turn on the mic, another poet got up and referenced the movie in the introduction to his poem. As he was reading his poem about gay marriage that bashed conservative Christians, I thought to myself, *I bet I get to follow this*. Sure enough when he sat down I was called up.

My poem was well received by the audience. The next poet was Michelle, who also referenced "The Passion of the Christ" in her introduction. She read a poem about suffering which questioned if Christ even existed. Later I had an opportunity to talk to her about her poem. We discussed the controversy surrounding the movie. She said she had fundamental questions about the historical accuracy of Scripture, but whenever she talked to Christians about it they got defensive and treated her as if she were ignorant. I shared the legitimacy of asking questions and gave her a book to read which addressed many of them. She responded by giving me a book that explained her worldview.

To show the spiritual diversity within the poetry community, one night I attended a writing workshop set up by a local youth organization. This particular week the workshop focused on memorization and performance. The students were asked to recite something from memory. People recited all kinds of things, mostly poems they had written. But some chose to recite prayers they had learned as children. Altogether there were prayers in four different languages from three major religions.

I was the "family man" poet who often wrote about my daughters, and they dubbed me "Big Poppa Shirk." Each time I was introduced Itchie Fingers, the DJ, would play the beat from Notorious B.I.G.'s, "Big Poppa". Eventually I was asked to be the weekly feature. The featured poet followed the open mic and was given 20–30 minutes to perform. I had fun preparing, and rewrote the lyrics to "Big Poppa". I dressed in baggy shorts, an oversized basketball jersey, sunglasses and "bling." I recruited Anacron who is a professional break-dancer to be my stunt double and provide the dance moves. The crowd loved seeing the "middle aged, family man" rapping away:

> *I'm a real dope rapper with a real fresh flow*
> *Spittin' rhymes up at ya from way down below*
> *So quit talkin' smack, get rid of your smirk*
> *Ain't nobody raps like the miniature Shirk*
> *I'm the Tip Top, of Hip Hop*
> *The midget MC that you can't stop*

Later I recruited another friend to play guitar while I sang the world's worst country music love song. I don't have a musical bone in my body, so achieving "world's worst" status was fairly easy. The guitar started playing and within three chords I was lost. So I sang louder, and I smiled bigger. Everyone loved it.

But the highlight of the evening for me was not my performance. It was what led up to it. The first poet on the open mic was Mama, who prefaced her poem by saying,

> Tonight we are in for a real treat. We have an authentic Christian for the feature. And he is actually worth hearing.

Later when Michelle got up to read her poem, she commented.

> Our feature tonight is the only person with an organized faith that I can get along with.

Finally the host got up and introduced me.

> Our feature tonight is a really great guy. If someday we stand at the gates of heaven, and our entrance depends upon what happened at our open mic, this guy is our only hope.

I thought I must have been doing something right. They had accepted me. I had earned the right to travel with them on this crazy journey through life.

chapter 5
the Sacrificial Poet arrives

Shortly after the Divine Poet spoke this world into existence
the poem was corrupted,
and the promise of Divine Intervention occurred

Centuries passed

The Divine Poet raised up poets to proclaim His poetry

But His poets reciting His Poetry were never enough

Divine Intervention required divinity

Humanity waited
Some like Simeon and Anna held on to belief
Others like Herod, had no time for the Divine Poet
But waited in hopes of stopping Divine Intervention
Claiming divinity for himself

As they waited they wondered
What would Divine Intervention look like?
How would the Divine Poet appear?
Would He come as a Conquering King
wielding weapons with divine might
crushing every foe?
Would He appear as a Wise Philosopher
enlightening the masses with His sage poetry?
Would He arrive as the Sovereign Judge
declaring His verdict
proclaiming the price men would pay for their
rebellion?

But everyone guessed wrong
He arrived not in a chariot descending from the clouds
but in the womb of a woman

Words etched on stone tablets had failed
So the Word became flesh.

Not powerful
  but powerless
Not speaking the wisdom of a sage
  but the incoherent babbling of an infant

Emptied of His Divine Glory
  so He could be filled with the frailty of humanity

And the waiting continued

While the Sacrificial Poet learned
  to walk
    talk
      and feed Himself

While He learned
  to be a man

Men had failed to listen when the Divine Poet spoke from the
  mountaintop

Now the Sacrificial Poet would teach them how to listen

By listening

To them

Listening as they taught him how to live with humanity

Before He could speak
  He had to listen.
Before He could teach
  He had to learn.

Those who desire to follow in His footsteps
  must take the same path.

Recently I was at the open mic at Weeds, which has a reputation for being pretty raw. It's not a place to go if you are easily offended. It's not uncommon to hear members of the audience heckle performers during their poem. Before the show started I was talking with the host. We met a couple of young ladies who said they were leaving Chicago to return home the next day. One of their goals for the trip was to read at an open mic and they had found out about Weed's on the Internet. During the show one of them got up and read a "Christian" poem. I was somewhat surprised. But I was not surprised when they left before the show was over, and the host commented on the mic about how we had listened to her but she wouldn't listen to us.

After the show ended I stayed to hang out with my friends at the bar. Soon the critique of her poem started, and I got to hear why everyone was offended by what she said.

> Who does she think she is, coming in here and preaching at us?

> How dare she talk like she knows what's wrong with us and how to fix it?

> I can't stand the arrogance of people like that.

Since becoming a regular member of Chicago's spoken word poetry scene, I have seen many poets cross the stage. Every once in while, another Christian shows up and shares their faith through poetry. Incarnational missions is a popular concept in the church, which sometimes results in Christian poets being "on mission" at an open mic.

Like the young lady at Weeds, most have not impressed me.

As the token Christian who has numerous conversations with poets about faith, I have become convinced that "drive by evangelism" is counterproductive. This caused me to look down on and judge "drive by evangelists". I was convinced they were not following in the footsteps of the Sacrificial Poet who became one of us to reach us.

I still believe in incarnational missions. But when I think of the incarnation of Jesus, I no longer just think of His birth. God became man. But becoming man involved much more than His birth. He wasn't born a man, at least, not a full grown mature man. He was born an infant. He had to learn how to become a man the same way all of us do. He listened to His parents. He mimicked His father. He looked up to people who were respected in the community. As strange as it may seem, Christ let mankind teach Him how to be a child of men, before He taught them how to be children of God. Paul sums up the incredible humility of Christ that allowed this to happen in Philippians 2:

> [5] Your attitude should be the same as that of Christ Jesus:

> [6] Who, being in very nature God,
>   did not consider equality with God something to be
>   grasped,
> [7] but made himself nothing,
>   taking the very nature of a servant
>   being made in human likeness.

> [8]*And being found in appearance as a man,*
> *he humbled himself*
> *and became obedient to death—*
> *   even death on a cross!*
> [9]*Therefore God exalted him to the highest place*
> *and gave him the name that is above every name,*
> [10]*that at the name of Jesus every knee should bow,*
> *in heaven and on earth and under the earth*
>
> [11]*and every tongue confess that Jesus Christ is Lord*
> *to the glory of God the Father.*

This has always been a favorite passage of mine. But I think most of my life I have missed a significant part of it. "Taking the very nature of a servant" was more than simply being born into the world. It involved serving as Joseph's apprentice, learning to be a carpenter. It involved being a child and learning to show proper respect for the people around Him. He did not have a sin nature to overcome, but He still had to learn obedience. He was born a perfect infant, but He had to learn what it was to be a perfect adult[2].

This was the first incarnational ministry. If we are to follow His example, we must learn to listen before we speak, to learn before we teach. If Christ's preparation for ministry took 30 years, we probably shouldn't rush into ours.

I am convinced incarnational ministry requires not just being there, but belonging there; not just going once as a visitor, but going regularly until you are adopted into the family.

But in my criticism of "drive by evangelists," the pendulum had begun to swing back.

It was much later that I realized just how far it had swung.

[2.] Hebrews 5:8–10 8*Although he was a son, he learned obedience from what he suffered* [9]*and, once made perfect, he became the source of eternal salvation for all who obey him* [10]*and was designated by God to be high priest in the order of Melchizedek.*

chapter 6

far from God

Maggot and I were hanging out at Cleo's bar talking about life and faith. I guess you could say I was trying to do incarnational ministry. He was the host of one of the open mics I regularly attended, but tonight we had just gotten together to talk. He had been raised by a Catholic mother, but had abandoned church. As the hours passed we covered topic upon topic. Around two in the morning, I mentioned to him how much I appreciated our conversations. He asked tough questions, and wouldn't settle for easy answers. Tough questions often become tests of faith. When the easy answers prove empty, you find out what kind of faith you really have. If faith isn't strong enough to handle tough questions, it has no value and I might as well be an atheist. Maggot stopped me mid-sentence.

> You think you'd be better off an atheist. John, you have no idea what it's like to be an atheist. To be wide-awake at three in the morning, and you know you have to be at work at six, but you can't sleep. All you can think about is what happens when you die. Is there really nothing more than being buried in the ground and eaten by worms?

I told him he was right. I have never had that experience, but if I was him, and I did, I would pray to the God I don't believe in. I'd tell God that if He is real, if He is there, I needed help. Maggot's response floored me. "John, don't you think I've had that conversation a thousand times."

I grew up thinking I could tell if a person was near to God, or on the verge of faith. Maggot would not have been someone I thought was on the verge of faith. He wasn't part of the evangelical culture I was raised in, and didn't express any interest in joining it. His involvement in the bar scene and the poetry community would have also seemed to put him far from God.

But those externals are the wrong way to judge. I look on the outward appearance, but the Sacrificial Poet looks on the heart. I see Maggot sitting at a bar and hear him read poetry at an open mic. The Sacrificial Poet sees the sleepless nights and hears the cries for help.

I'm convinced Maggot is closer to God than any of us realize, he's just far from the evangelical subculture I grew up in. As far as I know he has still not decided to follow Jesus, but I suspect someday he will. I think God's unlimited patience is at work in Maggot's life. I think he is close, but the last steps are often the hardest. I suspect that when Maggot finally chooses to follow Jesus, he will do so with a determination that will put me to shame. If I had to choose someone God is going to use to change the world, I might choose Maggot.

chapter 7

too broken for amazing grace

I was attending the Uptown Poetry Slam at Chicago's historic Green Mill, sitting with some friends at one of the round tables just a few feet from the stage. The evening featured two young ladies from out of state who performed music and poetry. In Chicago's spoken word poetry scene it is not uncommon for poets to showcase work that many Christians would find offensive, and this was one of those nights. One of the features had several pieces, which could best be described as "containing adult content." What made this night difficult for me was not the graphic content of the poetry. It was the fact that I was sitting in the front about eight feet away and at times throughout the evening, she looked directly at me and made me the object of her graphic comments. It wasn't that she was actually interested in me. She had no idea who I was. It was just part of her show.

I have never felt so uncomfortable in my life. I didn't know how to react. While the young lady did not know me, everyone at my table did. They knew I was the "token Christian," the "family man" with a wife and daughters. How is a Christian supposed to react? I suppose I could have got upset and left. I wasn't sure how that would advance the cause of Christ. I could have held up my left hand to show off my wedding ring, but I don't think that would have stopped her. She was already making similar comments to a lady friend of hers who was married and sitting a few seats away from me. I decided I probably couldn't stop her comments, and made it my goal to at least not encourage them. All I could do is sit there with an awkward, embarrassed look on my face.

I was relieved when the feature came to a close, until they started performing their encore. It was set to the tune of "Amazing Grace," but with lyrics about masturbation. Then they wrapped up by inviting the audience to sing the original lyrics to "Amazing Grace."[3] Over the course of my life I have probably been asked to join in singing

---

3. The one change in the lyrics was "saved a wretch like me" became "saved a Jew like me" a reference to one of the performers Jewish heritage. She had commented earlier in the evening about being Jewish and having "Jesus Envy."

"Amazing Grace" thousands of times. This was one time I couldn't. It hurt too much to hear a hymn that meant so much to me mocked. I sat silently while the rest of the audience sang.

It might be tempting to look down on them for singing a song that was hurtful to me as a follower of Christ. But I don't think they were trying to be hurtful. I suspect they were merely reflecting their culture, and I as an outsider was made uncomfortable. I have seen the same thing happen many times in churches, as pastors preached sermons that reflected their evangelical culture, and had no idea that what they said was hurtful to outsiders. The more I connected with my poet friends, the more critical I became of pastors who didn't seem to understand what they were communicating to people outside the church.

Later I found out the two ladies were going to feature at Mental Graffiti. I wanted to respond, not to be confrontational, but to remind my friends who knew I was a follower of Christ that there was more to Christianity than what had been portrayed that night.

I talked to some of the college students in my spiritual family who normally attended with me. I told them about the show at the Green Mill and suggested it was probably not a show they would want to attend. I asked them instead to meet together and pray for me as I tried to respond.

I signed up for the open mic, chose a seat away from the stage and waited to be called. I was nervous. I knew that after the open mic the feature was coming. I didn't know if they would choose to respond to my poem or not. But at the same time there was a feeling of calm. I felt convinced I was doing the right thing. I knew people were praying for me. I would have to trust God with the rest.

When I was called up I read, "What is Christianity?" (see Chapter 3). The audience clapped politely. The show went on. It was uneventful. The feature made no mention of my poem. At this show, they didn't sing "Amazing Grace." Maybe they weren't planning on it from the beginning.

Within two weeks I was discussing faith with Molly, who had been sitting at my table during the feature at the Green Mill. She was one of the most prominent poets in the Chicago Slam community. She had been raised in a church, but like many of my friends had been hurt deeply. I invited her to our spiritual family. She responded in an e-mail.

> *"I want to thank you for including me with this. I'll be out this friday, but I may be able to next friday. In spite*

of knowing you all, I'm a little nervous about reentering a Christian community again. I'm just not strong like I used to be, and I'm still very confused. I have a lot fear connected to faith, but I know you are all wonderful people and I'm thankful that you invited me to join."

Molly became a regular at our little gathering each Friday evening. She brought much to the group and was the person God used to teach me my next lesson.

One Friday evening she was unusually quiet. I could tell something was wrong as she occasionally got up to get a Kleenex. Afterwards I ask her if she was okay. She began to cry again, and retreated to the kitchen. I followed her, but quickly realized I needed help. So I went and got my wife, Amy. When Molly was ready to talk she said something I'll never forget.

"I'm not sure I can do this. I'm too broken. I'm not like you guys. You have such good hearts."

I didn't know what to say, so I said something stupid. Then Amy, whose college major was counseling, took over. The two of them went to sit on the couch while I said good-bye to the other guests. After everyone left, Amy asked me to clear the table. I took the hint and made myself busy in the kitchen. Later when I heard the two of them talking and laughing, I knew it was safe to return.

Not long after that, Molly's schedule changed at school. First it appeared to be a temporary conflict, but one thing led to another and she dropped out of the group.

My Christian friends might read this story and think it puts me in a good light. They might assume that Molly's words were a testament to my strong Christian testimony to my friends in the poetry scene. That I was shining a light in the darkness, and Molly was convicted of the sin in her life and unwilling to deal with it. They might even assume that the lesson to be learned is how to use your own life as a witness.

But they would be wrong. The real lesson was much less pleasant.

chapter 8

the greatest commandment

In Luke 10 the Sacrificial Poet said everything that matters can be summed up with two commands; love God and love your neighbor. A religious man in the audience immediately skipped over the first one and asked for clarification about the second. He needed to know who his neighbor was. Who was he required to love?

The Sacrificial Poet answered his question by telling the Parable of the Good Samaritan. For two thousand years, that parable has guided religious men in their understanding of how to love their neighbors.

But what of the greatest commandment? What about loving God? The religious man in Luke 10 didn't bother asking about it. I suspect he thought he already had that one covered. This is how religion works. Religious people assume they are fulfilling the command to love God by being religious.

But not according to the Sacrificial Poet. In the very next chapter He accused the most religious people of His day of neglecting justice and the love of God. [4]

This is how religion works. Religious people focus on religious things all the while failing to keep the greatest commandments.

But how does one keep the greatest commandment? What is the key to loving God? If it isn't being religious, what is it?

The Sacrificial Poet told another parable that holds the key. He was attending a dinner at the house of a Pharisee, when an immoral woman crashed the party. She was weeping uncontrollably, and began washing his feet with her tears, wiping them with her hair, kissing them, and pouring perfume on them.

As the disgusted host muttered under his breath, the Sacrificial Poet told a story.

> [41] *"Two men owed money to a certain money lender. One owed him five hundred denarii, and the other fifty.*

[4.] Luke 11:42

> [42]*Neither of them had the money to pay him back, so he canceled the debts of both. Now which of them will love him more?"*
>
> [43]*Simon replied, "I suppose the one who had the bigger debt canceled."*
>
> *"You have judged correctly," Jesus said.*[5]

Here is the key to fulfilling the greatest commandment. Here is the secret to loving God. We will only love God to the extent that we have been forgiven. The more we experience the forgiveness and grace of God, the more we will love Him. The deeper the pit we are rescued from, the deeper our love for Him will be. The immoral woman knew the depths of her brokenness. She loved much, for she had been forgiven much.

The host loved little, for he had never felt the need for forgiveness. He had lived a religious life and never fallen into gross immorality like the woman had, so he had never needed to be pulled from the pit.

Now back to Molly and me.

One of us was weeping.

One of us was broken.

One of us was religious.

[5] Luke 7:41–43

chapter 9

the least likely person

Our house church was studying the book of James. As we discussed James' warning against showing favoritism we decided to apply it to our efforts at prayer and evangelism. It is easy to judge people based on externals and then focus our efforts on those we are most comfortable with. Some people are easy to talk to, and fun to be around. They are a lot like us. They just need Jesus. Other people make us uncomfortable. They seem so far from God we want to give up even before we start. We decided to apply the passage from James by praying for the person we thought was least likely to respond to the gospel and follow Jesus.

This led to a fairly significant discussion. Who did we know who was the worst of sinners, the person who would take a miracle to reach? There were many possible choices, but eventually we settled on a young man named Morris Stegosaurus who seemed a very unlikely candidate for evangelism. He was a poet whose poetry was openly irreverent, irreligious, and even blasphemous. He was an atheist and didn't believe God existed. He was Jewish, so if God did exist, he was sure Jesus was not God. In addition to all this, he was openly gay and had a lifestyle that included things that even he would describe as aberrant.

But we started praying. We weren't at it for more than a few weeks when I came across Morris' online blog. The subject line was "Prayer," and it read like this:

> Lemme preface this by saying that I'm not trying to be an asshole. In fact, I'm making a conscious effort to not be an asshole.
>
> Also, I have a lot of respect for strong religious convictions. It may surprise you to learn that I have my own spiritual ideas as well, though I don't often discuss them (if you want to know, ask me privately sometime). So the point is that I'm not in any way making fun, okay?

So here's the thing:

I've seen a lot of people on lj talking about how they'll be praying for the people in New Orleans, and entreating others to also pray. What exactly is your perception of how prayer works?

What it's reading like to me is that you have this concept of a deity who is actively controlling a hurricane and aiming it at New Orleans. His intention is to do massive damage to New Orleans, and wipe out a lot of the population. So you pray. And you ask other people to pray. And what you're all doing, basically, is saying to God "Please don't let the hurricane hit New Orleans, or if you're gonna, please minimize the damage and loss of life".

So the idea, then, is that when God hears enough people saying that, he'll go "Okay, you convinced me. I'll mitigate the damage a little bit". Is that about it?

Because I'm seriously having trouble wrapping my head around that, on several levels. Am I not getting it?

Please explain.
I'm probably being in some respect obtuse, but I swear it's not deliberate. [6]

There were 27 comments from a wide variety of perspectives. Being an old guy who wasn't comfortable with Internet discussions (and being somewhat of a coward), I didn't try to comment. But I was amazed that our prayers were starting to be answered so quickly. The next time I saw Morris, I mentioned his blog. I told him he was asking some difficult questions. I said that as a follower of Christ who believed in prayer, I had to confess I had my own questions about prayer and how it worked. We had a great conversation. He did indeed have a strong respect for religious convictions. I was surprised to learn that he was a fan of C.S. Lewis and had read "The Chronicles of Narnia" as well as some of Lewis' other fictional works. C.S. Lewis has always been one of my favorite authors and I was able to loan him copies of a couple of books he had not read.

[6] Copyright Morris Stegosaurus, used by permission.

The conversation deepened our relationship. Later he announced at an open mic that he and his partner were moving to a new apartment, and needed help with the move. At this stage on my journey, this presented a dilemma. Like a good evangelical, I had to ask myself if I should help a gay couple move. As I thought about it, I realized that if a straight couple arrived next door and began to unload a truck, I wouldn't ask to see a marriage license and make moral judgments about their relationship before I offered to help. So I pulled the seats out of my minivan and volunteered to help.

It wasn't a difficult move, but Morris was very appreciative and thanked me with an invitation to his housewarming party. I wasn't sure how to react. It was an opportunity to get to know Morris better, but. . .should a good evangelical like me party with someone like Morris? I wasn't sure what partying with Morris would involve, but my imagination ran wild with images of alcohol, drugs, and pornography. I decided I had better have a talk with Morris before making my decision. So the next time I saw him, I told him I was flattered by the invitation, but I wasn't sure whether I should go. Was he sure he wanted a Christian at his party? I wouldn't want to ruin it. He said he definitely wanted me to come. I could be the "token Christian." These were the magic words. If I could be the token Christian at Mental Graffiti, why not be the token Christian at Morris's housewarming party?

I was still nervous about attending the party, but it was a "come and go" affair. I figured if anything got out of hand, I could leave. I loaded a platter full of my wife's famous chocolate chip cookies as a housewarming gift and off I went.

What a party! The majority of guests were gay, and true to his word every time someone new arrived, Morris introduced me as "John, our token Christian for the evening." This made me even more nervous. I was comfortable with my relationship with Morris. We had talked openly about faith, but I didn't know anyone else, and they didn't know me. I wondered what they thought when they heard me introduced as "our token Christian." What kind of stereotypes came to mind? Would I be labeled and judged before I even had a chance to make a first impression?

The introductions went much better than I expected. But I still felt like I was walking on eggshells. As the "token Christian" I knew that everything I said and did would reflect on Christ. Morris was a wonderful host, but one of his guests was not so wonderful, especially after he had been drinking awhile. I wasn't sure if his inappropriate behavior was normal for him, or if it was an intentional attempt to see how I would respond. Was I being tested? "Let's see how much this 'token Christian' can take." After he left several of the other guys commented on how his inappropriate behavior had bothered them as well, and I felt somewhat better.

At one point there were five of us at the party, two gay couples and myself. We were trying to figure out what to do when someone suggested we play a game. Morris pulled out Therapy The Game. I had never heard of it before, but he described it as Trivial Pursuit with a mental health twist. Instead of collecting pie pieces for answering questions about topics such as *Science and Industry* or *Arts and Leisure,* the goal was to collect colored pegs on your psychiatrist's couch, with each color representing the mental health issues faced during a different stage of life (infancy, childhood, adolescence, adulthood, seniority). As he described the game, I started getting nervous. It wasn't that the game sounded immoral or wrong. It would have probably been easier if it had been. If they had wanted to do drugs or watch pornography, I could have simply left. But this seemingly innocent game terrified me. I knew that as the "token Christian" my worldview was vastly different from anyone else playing the game. I thought of all the issues that would be really awkward to try to discuss, and as a follower of Christ I had to be honest in my answers. I determined to stay and play, and I silently offered up a quick prayer, *God, I'll play the game, if you shuffle the cards and watch the questions.*

So we started playing. The way you gain pegs in your couch is by serving as another player's therapist. The other player draws a card and writes down the answer to the question on a piece of paper. If you can correctly guess their answer, you get a colored peg representing that topic. To give you an example, Morris drew a card with the question, "Which of the people playing this game is most likely to be harboring a deep dark secret?" As he wrote down his answer to be guessed, he made some cryptic comments about deep, dark secrets to his friend who was serving as his therapist. His therapist guessed that the one with the secret was probably John, the token Christian. Morris revealed that he had guessed correctly, and commented that it couldn't be one of them. As messed up as they were, their darkness wasn't secret. Everything was out in the open. If there was anyone harboring a deep, dark secret, it had to be the "token Christian" who appeared to be happily married with a wife and kids.

We all chuckled and the game went on.

No one knew that Morris' words would rock my world and change my life forever.

chapter 10

the Sacrificial Poet exposes the deep dark secrets

The Sacrificial Poet was a friend of sinners. At least, He was a friend of sinners who knew they were sinners. He came to heal the sick, but only those who knew they were sick could enjoy His healing touch.

This caused grave distress to the Pharisees, the religious conservatives of His day. They wanted sinners judged and were sure that sickness was proof of sin. With a quick look they could tell who measured up. The tax collectors and sinners were tearing apart the moral fabric of society. Fornicators and adulterers were a threat to traditional family values. They were locked in a culture war for the heart and soul of society.

But the heart and soul of society were precisely what they couldn't see. They could only judge externals.

But that was enough. They had no trouble determining who was least likely to follow the sacred poetry of the Divine Poet. But in as much as they studied, and memorized that poetry, when the Word became flesh, and the Sacrificial Poet walked among them, they failed to recognize Him.[7]

As the tax collectors, the sinners, the prostitutes, and all the least likely people fell down to worship the Sacrificial Poet, the Pharisees stood in judgment.

They judged the tax collectors.

They judged the sinners.

They judged the prostitutes.

They judged the Sacrificial Poet.

But they failed to look into their own hearts and grapple with their own deep dark secrets.

But the Sacrificial Poet knew the deep dark secrets in the hearts of men. He knew that true judgment begins on the inside.

[7.] John 5:39–40 You diligently study the Scriptures because you think that by them you possess eternal life. These are the Scriptures that testify about me, yet you refuse to come to me to have life.

The Sacrificial Poet exposed the secret. The least likely people, the greatest sinners were not the tax collectors and prostitutes, but the Pharisees[8].

Morris may have thought he was joking, and I'm sure Molly thought she was the broken one and I had a good heart. But that's how secrets work. The deep dark secret was that I am an arrogant Pharisee. It was arrogant of me to think I could determine who was the least likely person to follow Christ. It was wrong of me to base my judgment on externals rather than the heart. If I am to take the words of Christ seriously, I must conclude that the least likely person to follow Christ is not a sinner on the outside looking in, but a church-going Pharisee who sings in the choir, serves on the deacon board, and polishes the outside of the cup to a bright sheen, all the while harboring an evil heart that rejects the truth.

I am a Pharisee. I washed the outside of the cup so that Molly would think I had a good heart. I was sure I could tell the condition of Morris' heart by looking at the externals.

As a result, I robbed Molly of hope. Had she known the truth about how broken I was on the inside, and seen the grace and mercy of God at work healing my brokenness, she could have seen that grace truly is greater than all our sin.

Morris saw through my hypocrisy, or at least he saw the possibility of my hypocrisy, but I still robbed him of seeing the grace of God. He didn't see the wretchedness of my heart being healed by the grace of God. He just saw the possibility that I was a hypocrite like so many other Christians he knew. Hypocrisy doesn't draw people to Jesus.

If I am to show people the way to Jesus, I must be on the way to Jesus. The only way to Jesus is the way of brokenness. Until I can see how unlikely my own salvation is, I will not experience what it is to be truly forgiven and pulled from the depths of hell. Until in despair I cry out for mercy, and receive it, I will not be capable of loving God with all my heart.

But I did all that as a small child. I prayed the sinner's prayer. That should have taken care of it.

Right?

[8.] Matthew 21:31b-32 I tell you the truth, the tax collectors and the prostitutes are entering the kingdom of God ahead of you. For John came to you to show you the way of righteousness, and you did not believe him, but he tax collectors and prostitutes did. And even after you saw this, you did not repent and believe him.

chapter 11
a least likely sacrificial poet

Saul was a Pharisee
Waiting for the intervening hand of God

A foot soldier in the culture war
  Inflicting mass casualties on the enemy

A proud man
  Proud that he wasn't like the men he fought
  Proud of how well he fought

He could spot the least likely person a mile away
One look brought
  condemnation,
    judgment
      and hate

He quoted Greek poets, but despised the Sacrificial Poet

Until a light shone into his blindness
  Opening his eyes to the Truth

The Sacrificial Poet was the Intervention he had waited for

Instantly surrendering
He laid down his weapons

And became a sacrificial poet
  Following his Leader
    Proclaiming His Poetry

But his battles had not ended
He merely switched sides

Having seen the cesspool of his soul
  The darkest secrets of his own heart
He was his own enemy
An enemy he fought
  with all the weakness he could muster
But weakness
  was all he could muster

Until the least likely person
Learned to stop fighting
And surrender to the Sacrificial Poet
Moment by moment
Day by day

When I moved to Chicago, I wanted to be like the Apostle Paul. He was a cross-cultural missionary who was used by God to transform the world. He lived an exciting life starting churches in exotic places.

Ten years have passed. I have not transformed the world. I have a small group that meets in my home. Hardly Paul-like.

At least not in the ways I wanted to be. I am like Paul in all the wrong ways. I'm like the Paul who came to realize the pride in his heart was worse than the external sins he condemned men for.

I'm like the Paul who finally recognized the least likely person.

When he looked in a mirror.

I can confidently say with Paul:

> [15]*Here is a trustworthy saying that deserves full ac-*
> *ceptance: Christ Jesus came into the world to save*
> *sinners—of whom I am the worst.* [16]*But for that very*
> *reason I was shown mercy so that in me, the worst*
> *of sinners, Christ Jesus might display his unlimited*
> *patience as an example for those who would believe*
> *on him and receive eternal life. (1 Timothy 1:15–16)*

Note the present tense. Paul does not write that he was the worst, before he was saved when he was persecuting Christians and applauding while Stephen was stoned to death. Paul writes, "I am the worst." Even near the end of his life, Paul was acutely aware of the wretchedness of his own heart.

And this is a trustworthy saying that I, too, can accept. "Christ Jesus came into the world to save sinners—of whom I am the worst." My sin did not end when I prayed the sinner's prayer as a child. To this very day I wrestle with the evil lurking in the depths of my heart. I need to repent daily and experience forgiveness if I am to grow in my love for God and fulfill the greatest commandment. The Sacrificial Poet chose me because I am the least likely person. He also chose me because

I am sinful, weak and foolish[9]. But in His unlimited patience he offers me mercy. His grace is healing my brokenness, causing my love for Him to grow.

I owe Molly an apology. I don't have a good heart. Just a good mask.

I owe Morris one, too. My mask was covering more than my evil heart. It also hid the grace, mercy, and unlimited patience of God at work in my life.

[9.] 1 Corinthians 1 [26]*Brothers, think of what you were when you were called. Not many of you were wise by human standards; not many were influential; not many were of noble birth.* [27]*But God chose the foolish things of the world to shame the wise; God chose the weak things of the world to shame the strong.* [28]*He chose the lowly things of this world and the despised things—and the things that are not—to nullify the things that are,* [29]*so that no one may boast before him.* [30]*It is because of him that you are in Christ Jesus, who has become for us wisdom from God—that is, our righteousness, holiness and redemption.* [31]*Therefore, as it is written: "Let him who boasts boast in the Lord."*

chapter 12
their God who hates me

Tristan is a Jewish lesbian and phenomenal spoken word artist. I remember listening to her perform a poem with the following lines at an open mic.

forgiveness is what jesus gives.
salvation is what i'm after.
hell is a hotel.

but i don't think god exists.
even if he did,

this place holds all the souls god turned his back on. we sit in the center of satan's palm together and wait for jesus to return.

oh yeah, i pray now.
it's this new addition to my life.
it came out of my head like a limb.
i pray to the back god turned on me.

i pray and then take a shower.
i take a shower and then pace.
i pace and then write.
i write and then cry.
i cry and then pray.

but i don't believe my voice so i tell myself i can't die yet. my prayers have to at least sound genuine before i go[10]

As she sat down DJ Itchie Fingers, who always seems to pick the perfect music, played an old Belinda Carlisle song I remembered from my teen years. The lyrics really hit me.

They say in heaven love comes first
We'll make heaven a place on earth[11]

[10.] Copyright Tristan Silverman, used by permission all rights reserved. This is a draft of a poem that was frequently edited and never finished.
[11.] *"Heaven is a Place on Earth"* written by Rick Nowels & Ellen Shipley

After the open mic ended I talked to Tristan about her piece. I mentioned that while the two of us had very little in common when it comes to our beliefs about God and theology, I thought her piece was powerful, and I appreciated hearing her honest struggle. I was shocked when she summed up the difference between us this way.

> *"John, you are what happens when God fills you, I am what happens when he empties you."*

I told her that recently God had been teaching me the importance of being emptied. As our talk ended, I asked if she would be willing to have lunch with Amy and me and continue the conversation. She said she would.

We made plans for her to come over, but before the day came, she called and asked if she could bring a friend who was visiting from out of state. I told her that would be fine, but I wondered how it would affect our ability to talk about faith. My anxiety only increased when she arrived and introduced me to her friend Tina, who was the founder and director of a nonprofit center for queer writers. Faith is an intensely intimate topic, which I prefer to discuss in the context of a personal relationship, especially when dealing with people from subcultures and lifestyles historically at odds with the church such as the gay and lesbian community. They often carry deep wounds inflicted on them by people who claimed to speak for Christ. As a result they can be defensive or even antagonistic towards Christianity. I told Amy that I wasn't going to try to force a conversation about faith. The goal was simply to build a relationship and show them love. We would be good hosts and attempt to show them that not all stereotypes about Christians are true.

But I was hardly into my third spoonful of soup when Tristan started asking about faith. Before I knew it our guests were sharing their own experiences as they struggled to live in a broken world and find healing for their brokenness. They even spoke about seeking to come to terms with the sin in their lives and understand forgiveness. As I shared my struggle with what it means to follow Christ in the city, and my understanding of the love of Christ which was poured out in grace and forgiveness in my own life, they listened intently. To give you an idea of their immense pain, when I mentioned my belief that the church was the family of God and should function like a family, Tina commented,

> *I don't believe in family anymore. At least, I don't believe in the permanence of family. I think the safety*

and comfort of family is something that may happen for short periods of time, but then it's gone. At least, that is where I am right now. Maybe someday I will believe in it again, but right now I am afraid to.

Those words stung. How does one respond to such a statement? As I thought about it later, I couldn't help but thank God for my parents and grandparents who showed me that with God's help, a family can be a permanent, safe place.

The next day Tina was the feature at an open mic I attended. I read a poem about how faith is living when you don't have all the answers, and how God chooses messed up people like me [12]. During the feature Tina dedicated her last poem to me. She said it was related to the conversation we had over lunch. It contained lines about her uncle and aunt and "their God who hates me." After the show I talked with her about the poem, and told her simply "my God doesn't hate you." Her initial response was "Oh, yes I know that from our conversation yesterday." Then she stopped for a second and said, "Thank you, no one's ever told me that before." I apologized to her and felt like weeping. How had we gotten so far from John 3:16, "For God so loved THE WORLD"? Then in reference to my poem she added, "If you are going to keep passing out redemption, you should quit saying you suck." To which I replied, "No, that wouldn't be true. I do suck. That's the point." The secret was out.

[12.] See "Why I Believe" in the Epilogue

chapter 13

the Sacrificial Poet weeps

The Sacrificial Poet wept
* For a world of poor people*
*   hurting people*
*   sinful people*
*   losers*
He wept out of love
He lived out that love
And they loved him
But not all of them
There were the rich and powerful,
* the religious elite*
They were winners
They didn't need him
And they didn't love
Not "those people"
But He befriended "those people"
* the poor*
* the homeless*
* criminals*
* prostitutes*
* the underbelly of society*
The religious elite were outraged
* "He should know better"*
* "Those people are sinners"*
* "Sinners must be condemned"*
* "Guilty by association," they said*
* "Why would a good man hang out with hookers?"*
* "There's only one reason to hang out with hookers"*
* "A good man wouldn't"*
But the Sacrificial Poet was different
He loved people
Even "those people"
Even hookers
And as he loved
"Those people" flocked to him

Scaring the rich, powerful, religious elite
Their power threatened
They had to act
So they killed him
Made a public spectacle of his execution
That should end the madness
But the madness didn't end
There were reports that He lived again
That He was seen alive by. . . "those people"
And "those people" changed
They began to love like He loved
That love changed the world
"Those people" circled the globe
Known for their love
The rich and powerful couldn't stop "those people"
Until "those people" became rich and powerful
And a new religious elite was born
And love was lost,
And the poor didn't matter,
And sinners were condemned,
And once again,
The Sacrificial Poet wept

chapter 14

am i a hater?

I have no idea if Belinda Carlisle knows the Sacrificial Poet. I know she isn't a Christian music artist. I can remember as a kid hearing about the dangers of secular music. At times I was convinced that everything secular was evil. I enjoyed secular music but felt guilty about it. I didn't think Christians were allowed to listen to Belinda Carlisle. Now I'm quoting her in my book. I guess I've come to the conclusion that sometimes pop music and slam poetry get things right. If Paul could quote the pagan poets of his day, I suppose I can quote Belinda Carlisle or Eitan Kadosh. I'm trying to learn not to condemn people or things simply because they reside outside the evangelical culture I grew up in.

But back to Belinda's theology. In heaven does love come first? For the Sacrificial Poet taught the greatest commandment was "Love God", and the second was "Love your neighbor." So I guess you could say that in heaven, love comes first. . .and second.

But should we make heaven a place on earth? Avoiding the complicated eschatological arguments that I don't claim to understand, the commandments to love were given for the present, not just the future, and the Sacrificial Poet taught us to pray, "your kingdom come, your will be done on earth as it is in heaven."[13] If God who is love indwells us, and we love our neighbors, won't we be bringing a piece of heaven to earth?

But that is not what Tristan and Tina saw when they looked at the church. Tristan saw a God who had turned His back on her. Tina saw a God who hates her. I know that God has done neither of those things. So where did they get these ideas?

Maybe from Pharisees like me.

We turn our backs on the people around us. And yes, sometimes we hate. We don't think we hate sinners. We hate what they do. "Hate the sin, love the sinner." But I've noticed a problem. I treat people inside the church different from people on the outside. I once had a pastor

---

[13.] Matthew 6:10

who experienced a moral failure that cost him his ministry. I hated his sin, but I loved him. For months my wife and I made sure there was someone to baby-sit his kids each week while he and his wife went to counseling and saved their marriage. I focused so much on trying to love him that some people might have thought I was being soft on sin.

But people outside the church are different. I am more likely to focus on hating their sin than loving them. It is easy to denounce their sin. The temptation to be a culture warrior rears its ugly head. And the warrior in me finds it difficult to love my enemies.

This is a problem with culture wars. It is easier to fight enemies than love them. What we call hating sin is often seen as hating sinners. They see Christians chanting slogans and carrying picket signs outside abortion clinics. They hear evangelicals denouncing same sex marriage and signing petitions to defeat them politically. Then we explain that we love them. And the words ring hollow.

Maybe they are hollow. While hatred can be communicated in one sentence; love is an action. Love has to be lived out. Yet too often we live out our hatred of sin, and try to convince them of our love with mere words.

This is a formula for failure.

So I have determined. It is more important for people to know that I love them, than for them to know what I think about their sin.

chapter 15

the lost words of the Sacrificial Poet

She stood there wrapped in a blanket
Pulled from a bed of illicit passion
Embarrassed
Humiliated
Guilty

Her accusers clutched chunks of granite
Ready to uphold the law
Young children were sent away
They mustn't see what would take place
Older ones were forced to watch
Let this be an example, a warning

They presented her to the Sacrificial Poet
To pronounce judgment
But He just bent down
Put His finger to the sand
And began to write

They became impatient
"You know the Law,"
"She must die"

He interrupted His inscription
"Let the one without sin throw the first stone"
Again He wrote

They looked at each other thinking
"He agrees she should be stoned"
"But who goes first?"
No one dared presume perfection

But they had heard rumors about this Poet
That He had no sin
Maybe He wanted the honor for Himself
Someone tried to hand Him a rock
He just kept writing
One by one, stones dropped

The mob grew still
One by one, accusers left

Until the cowering woman looked up
And saw only one man
The only one qualified to judge
The only one qualified to condemn
The only one who could throw the first stone

"Where are they? Has no one condemned you?"
He spoke softly
"No one, sir," she quivered
"Then neither will I, Go and sin no more"

Two thousand years later
Men wonder
What did He write?
For the Sacrificial Poet spoke often
But wrote only once
But the one time He wrote
He wrote powerful words
Dispersing a mob
Dispensing mercy

What were those words?
No one knows
For when He finished writing
There was no one left to read them
Except a teary eyed woman

Who apparently told no one
The words of the Poet
Who gave her
A second chance

chapter 16

soft on sin?

But is focusing on loving sinners, even at the expense of confronting sin, being soft on sin?

I think it is all about timing. When the woman caught in adultery was brought before Christ, He didn't rush to confront her sin. That might have resulted in a mob lynching.

Instead, He showed love and spared her life.

Then He refused to condemn her.

Then He told her to "Go and sin no more."

Maybe I should follow in his footsteps. Love first. Refuse to condemn. Then share the truth about sin.

But for me, I think there might be an additional step. After all, He was the sinless Sacrificial Poet who was qualified to throw the first stone. I am just a Pharisee who often wants to throw the first stone.

I once heard someone speculate that when Jesus stooped to write in the sand, He wrote out the concealed sins of each man who stood ready to stone the woman caught in adultery. I know it's speculation, but I like to think that's what happened. Everyone was ready to condemn her, until they saw the deep dark secrets of their hearts written out in the sand.

That's why the stones dropped.

I wonder how I would confront sin if each conversation about sin started with a discussion of my own?

I think my stones would drop.

Maybe I would focus on loving people without worrying about confronting their sin. This is what I'm trying to do. I point people to Jesus who has grace, mercy and unlimited patience. But sooner or later the topic of sin comes up. Often they ask the question, "What do you think about. . .?" You can fill in the blank with something they find near and dear to their heart. They want to know if I will condemn them like other

Christians they have encountered. And believe me, other Christians have condemned them. Tristan told me a story of a total stranger who told her she was going to hell solely based on her appearance.

I am convinced that often they aren't really asking me if they are a sinner. Most people know they are a sinner, even if they don't define sin the way I do. No one measures up to his or her own moral standard. What they are really asking is, "Is my sin unforgivable?"

They want to know if God hates them.

So I tell them about an assignment I had to do in a seminary class. I had to look up every passage of Scripture that deals with pride, arrogance, and humility, including all the forms of each word. It was a long assignment. By the time I was done, I was convinced that pride is the worst of sins. It was the sin of Satan who wanted to be like the Most High. Pride was part of the serpent's temptation of Eve in the garden when he told her that she could know good and evil like God. When Ezekiel listed the sins of Sodom, which resulted in divine judgment, arrogance tops the list.[14]

Pride is also my sin. It's what makes me the least likely person to follow Jesus. According to Ezekiel, I have no business calling anyone else a "sodomite." Pot, meet kettle.

But there is good news. The Sacrificial Poet loves lost causes. He chooses weak, foolish, sinful people. He is displaying His unlimited patience in my life by pouring out grace and mercy. His strength is overcoming my weakness. His sacrifice was enough to provide forgiveness even for my pride.

I point out that it's dangerous for me to focus on other people's sin. I'm still trying to get the log out of my own eye so I can see clearly to help them with the speck in theirs.

And it's really hard to get the log out of my eye when I've got a stone in my hand.

After I have been as honest as I can about the ugliness of my own heart.

After I have dropped the stones.

[14.] Ezekiel 16:49–50 *49"'Now this was the sin of your sister Sodom: She and her daughters were arrogant, overfed and unconcerned; they did not help the poor and needy. 50They were haughty and did detestable things before me. Therefore I did away with them as you have seen.*

I begin to answer their question. Yes, I believe you are a sinner. But not an unforgivable one. I'm proof.

The key to not being soft on sin is not being soft on my sin.

chapter 17

who wants to be a conversion project?

part 1

Lee and Susan lived next door. They introduced me to Chicago's anarchist subculture. While anarchism probably leads many to think of violence and revolution, the anarchists we met were great people. They had an equal disdain for capitalism, socialism, and communism. They were against all forms of authority since, to quote Lord Acton, "Power tends to corrupt, and absolute power corrupts absolutely." But they cared deeply for justice and the rights of the poor and oppressed. While I disagreed with some of their ideas, I grew to respect much about them. For example, they cared more for people than things. Money and material things didn't seem to matter much. I remember a birthday party at Lee and Susan's with a bunch of their anarchist friends. Several of us sat in the backyard with our feet soaking in a kiddie pool that someone had found discarded in an alley. I don't think anyone brought presents. People did bring food, but it didn't appear they stressed about it. They just brought whatever they had. I remember someone brought a partial carton of eggs. It was the first (and only) time I ever saw someone grill an egg on a barbecue while it was still in the shell. No one had to impress anyone. No one had to wear masks.

Lee and Susan saw the church as an oppressive force in the world, but respected Jesus. In their eyes, Jesus was an anarchist. He spoke truth to power, and didn't get caught in the political power struggles of His day. He cared for the poor and oppressed. To Lee and Susan this stood in stark contrast to the American church.

They never joined the Friday night gatherings where our spiritual family met to share a meal, discuss a passage of Scripture and pray for each other. But they did get involved in some of our community service projects. One summer we discovered one of the local parks was understaffed, a common occurrence in the city. As a result, there was no one to empty the trashcans on the weekends when the park was full of patrons. Our group decided to meet at the park every Sunday to have a picnic and serve the community by emptying the garbage cans. Lee and Susan were there to help every week.

As summer was winding down, I remember a conversation regarding our plans for the fall. I mentioned that we might have some college students from Moody Bible Institute joining us each week. I was surprised when they became very concerned.

> *Moody Bible Institute, we've heard about Moody Bible Institute. Aren't they evangelical, right-wing homophobes? I'm not sure we can work with evangelical, right-wing homophobes.*

I tried to alleviate their concern.

> *They are evangelicals and they do tend to be politically conservative, and they probably believe that homosexuality is wrong. But these Sunday picnics aren't about politics or sexual orientation. They are about serving the community of Wicker Park. We serve because Jesus said, "Love your neighbor." I don't think there will be a problem. If anyone displays hatred of any group of people we won't tolerate it.*

They seemed to accept this, and I thought I was out of the woods, until the question came.

> *You aren't trying to proselytize are you? I don't think I want to be a conversion project.*

chapter 18

evil evangelism?

I once did a survey in Wicker Park for a class I was taking. I asked a young man if he believed in absolute truth. He confidently said, "No, everyone has their own truth. What's true for you is true for you. What's true for me is true for me." I told him I believe in absolute truth. His response, "That's true for you."

Anyone who has been through an apologetics class has heard the arguments about absolute versus relative truth. It's a "gotcha" trap that Christians use when they are debating people outside the church. Yet this man didn't feel "got." He had no problem with the notion that the two of us had competing, contradictory truths, and that we both were right.

In fact, in our culture, one of the most offensive things you can say to someone is, "You are wrong."

Which, unfortunately, is how I used to frame the debate.

Nobody likes being proselytized. Think about it. Proselytizing begins with the assumption that something is wrong with you, and I know how to fix it. Often it shows a lack of respect.

This flies in the face of some of the most cherished values of our society like tolerance, diversity, and multiculturalism. Our culture wants to believe that all religions are equal and everyone has a right to their own truth.

Most Christians struggle with evangelism. We don't like it anymore than the people we target. We listen to sermons, read books and take classes. We learn all kinds of methods, but we rarely use them. When we muster up the courage to try, we rarely get the results we want. This leaves us feeling like guilty failures.

If you think I'm being harsh, do a survey of the churches in your community and see what their rate of growth by conversion is. If the goal is converting our friends, most of us aren't doing well. There are exceptions, but for every "gifted evangelist" among us, there are several more frustrated failures. We feel guilty that we aren't sharing our faith enough. Then when we muster up the courage to try we don't see the results we want and wonder what is wrong.

If Christ who has all authority has sent us out to make disciples, with the promise that He goes with us,[15] why isn't it working?

The easy excuse is to blame the people who refuse to be converted.

> I was faithful to give the gospel. They refused to listen. Why should we be surprised when terrible sinners reject Christ? It's hardly likely that someone so sinful would repent. They must have really hard hearts.

I suppose this is a possible explanation, but it also sounds a lot like the Pharisee in me is surfacing again.

So I am tempted to go from blaming them to blaming us.

I once heard someone say the best method of evangelism is the one you use. I'm not so sure. I think some evangelism is counter productive. Some is even evil. I began to wonder about this when I saw how my friends were offended and even pushed away from Christ by Christians who tried to proselytize them.

When I looked at Scripture I became convinced.

> [1]If I speak in the tongues of men and of angels, but have not love, I am only a resounding gong or a clanging cymbal. [2]If I have the gift of prophecy and can fathom all mysteries and all knowledge, and if I have a faith that can move mountains, but have not love, I am nothing. [3]If I give all I possess to the poor and surrender my body to the flames, but have not love, I gain nothing.[16]

Without love all my attempts at godliness are worthless and without merit. I suspect this includes my attempts at evangelism.

Maybe love does come first.

Maybe if he were preaching to today's philosophers. Paul would quote Belinda Carlisle.

[15.] See the Great Commission in Matthew 28:18–20
[16.] 1 Corinthians 13

chapter 19

who wants to be a conversion project?

part 2

When we ended chapter 17, Lee and Susan wanted to know if I was trying to convert them. They made it clear they did not want to be proselytized. They were people not projects.

How is a missionary supposed to respond to that? I suppose I could have written them off as hard hearted, and then moved on to my next conversion project. But they were my neighbors and I already cared about them. They were more than a project.

So I reminded them of our many conversations about politics and anarchism. I pointed out that I knew they sincerely believed their ideas would make the world a better place. I knew they would love to see me convert and embrace anarchism and join their struggle to bring about a better world where justice prevailed and people's lives were improved.

In a sense, I was their conversion project.

But I didn't mind because I knew they respected me as a friend, and allowed me to make up my own mind. In fact, their belief in anarchism was inconsistent with manipulating or forcing people to convert. I knew our relationship did not depend upon me changing my beliefs.

I told them that like the Moody students, I was an evangelical from a right wing background, but living in Chicago God had been teaching me what really mattered was to follow the teachings of Christ to love God and love my neighbors. I sincerely believed that Jesus is the only way to transform people's lives and bring about a better world, and I would love to see more of my friends (including them) come to share my beliefs and experience the life that Jesus offers, but love left no place for manipulation or coercion.

They commented again that they had no problem with Jesus or His teachings. It was the church, hypocritical Christians, and organized religion they feared, distrusted and disliked.

A few days later Susan shared with me that she recognized her opinion of Christians was based upon stereotypes. She realized Jesus didn't fit those stereotypes and said maybe she would like to follow Jesus if she could do it without being a Christian.

chapter 20

who wants to be a christian?

Could Susan follow Jesus without being a Christian? Before we try to answer that, I should point out that this way of thinking is not uncommon. Many people today are attracted to the teachings of Jesus but repulsed by something they have seen or experienced within Christianity. They see Jesus as loving and accepting, but His followers as hateful, intolerant bigots.

Our initial reaction is to disagree with their definitions and argue with them about what the word Christian really means. But I am afraid that such arguments have no winners. Usually their beliefs are based upon their personal experience, and our words alone can't change that. If their opinion of Christianity was forged when they were deeply wounded by someone wearing the label "Christian," they probably want nothing to do with "Christians."

We can try to explain that not all Christians are like that, and give examples of Christians who are following Jesus and carrying out His mission in the world by loving their neighbors, feeding the hungry, and healing the sick. But either they won't believe us, and we've gained nothing, or they will believe us and we run the risk of robbing them of hope. If Christians are such good people, and have such good hearts, maybe they can never measure up.

I'm beginning to think we should just agree with them.

Aren't they really saying that Jesus loves the world, but Christians are the worst of sinners? That's a pretty good description of Him (at least it's a good start), and a pretty good description of me.

If someone is interested in following Jesus but critical of the Christians, maybe we should point out that Christians are people who need Jesus, too.

Most people outside the church recognize this. They see the church's flaws better than we do. They know we don't measure up to the standard that Christ set.

Occasionally, I am invited to speak at churches. I have found one of the best ways to talk to my friends about Jesus is to talk to them about what I am planning to say. I have had friends in Chicago tell me I am their missionary to the church. They encourage me to go tell the Christians how to follow Jesus, because they are convinced most Christians aren't doing a very good job.

I remember another conversation with Lee at a coffee shop. I don't remember how, but the topic turned to a prominent Christian leader who had recently passed away. Lee told me he was convinced that if hell existed it surely contained an extra fiery place for this man and men like him.

What's a guy to do? Lee's knowledge of this individual was limited to things he had seen in the media, which were often hostile and probably biased. I could try to reeducate him and tell him about the good things the man had also done, but the last thing I wanted to do was be forced to argue with Lee about the character and reputation of a man neither of us knew personally. We would both be parroting things we had heard from others, and ultimately what would be gained?

Instead I used the opportunity to talk about Jesus. I told Lee I didn't believe that admission to heaven and hell are based on how good or bad we are, but on the work of Christ. Without Jesus, the man in question would surely be in hell, but if he had come to Christ for forgiveness, the grace of God was enough to rescue sinners even of his magnitude.

I think that is the core of the gospel. Not that Christians are good people, but that God's grace can save bad people.

If God's grace can reach people as bad as me, no one is without hope.

chapter 21

conversions or conversations

Jeff is a transgender, neo-Viking pagan who worships Loki the Viking god of mischief and fire. One night I arrived early to the open mic. When Jeff saw me, he immediately grabbed my arm and pulled me from the room saying, "I've been waiting for you, I need advice from a godly man!" I missed most of the show, as I spent the entire night talking to Jeff and the roommate he had been having problems with. Later in the evening I was able to pray with Jeff for the first time.

Arriving early at another open mic, I sat down next to the host, Gregorio and he told me he had been thinking about me. He was raised Catholic, and had left the church years ago, but recently got a job working security at the cathedral downtown. He said the mass usually bores him, but this week during the homily the speaker talked about friendship. He said that sometimes God enriches our lives with the most unexpected friends who show up at the most unexpected places. Gregorio said he immediately thought of me. In fact, he said he looked toward heaven and asked, "Are you trying to get my attention?" I smiled at him and said, "Wow, it sounds like He is trying to get your attention. You better be careful. You can run but you can't hide." We continued talking. Gregorio made it clear that he was not planning on converting, but he was comfortable discussing faith with me.

As Christians we often think our mission is to convert people. There is a problem with this. We can't convert anyone. Conversion is between God and the individual. If we try to take responsibility for things we can't control, we are doomed to frustration. Fortunately our mission is not converting others; it is allowing God to fully convert us so we can be His hands and feet living out His love for the world and speaking the message of Good News. I would love to see Jeff and Gregorio come to know the love and healing that reconciliation with God brings, but I can't make that happen. To this day both of them assure me they are not going to change their beliefs. Jeff just appreciates that I was there as a friend to listen to him and pray with him while he went through a difficult time. Gregorio considers me a friend who has enriched his life. Their conversion is out of my control, and it shouldn't be my focus. What I can control is how I live my life.

Will I love my neighbor, and be an unexpected friend who shows up in an unexpected place, or will I stay away from people like Jeff and Gregorio and the places where they spend their time?

Will I live out my struggle to follow Jesus before people like Jeff so they can see God at work in my life?

Will have a listening ear and allow wisdom from God's Word to be evident in my life so that I become a person who is sought out during difficult times?

Will I be a "token Christian" in their circle of friends?

And it's not just about what I might do for them. That is only half the equation. God wants to enrich my life through unexpected friends in unexpected places, friends like Morris, Molly, Jeff and Gregorio.

Will I be humble enough to let Him? Humble enough to be not just a teacher but a student?

chapter 22

between two worlds

When I first moved to Chicago the goal was to take Jesus to the city. Jesus was a "friend of sinners" and I thought the city was the obvious place to find sinners He could befriend. Now I realize how arrogant that was. Jesus didn't need me to take Him to the city. Jesus was already there. When white evangelicals fled the city for the suburbs He stayed behind. It also rarely crossed my mind that if Jesus was a friend of sinners, and I was His friend. . . .

This arrogance was fed when I spoke at churches and had people praise me for doing ministry in what they perceived as a difficult setting.

It is also fed by my identity as the "token Christian" at the open mics I attend. When my friends in the poetry scene assume I am one of "the good Christians," or tell me how terrible Christians are "present company excepted," I feel pretty good about myself. When they suggest I tell Christians about Jesus, because they need to hear it, I puff up a little.

Living between two worlds is awkward. You can feel homeless, not quite comfortable in either one, and afraid of the chasm that separates them. But pride makes it easier. All you have to do is imagine you have one foot on each world. Now assume you are a giant who can stand tall and look down on them both. If it helps, you can place yourself on a pedestal for an even better view of all the messed up broken people below.

chapter 23

overreacting

I grew up in the church. It was a good church too. I built meaningful relationships with people who cared for me. After graduating from high school I attended a good Christian college. Later I went to seminary with the goal of working in a church. I was not just an evangelical; I was an evangelical who was training to lead evangelicals. I remember in seminary being told by a pastor that he would love to have me come work at his church when I graduated, but he was sure I would end up at a much larger one.

But something happened after years of connecting with the poets of Chicago. I changed. I stopped attending traditional churches and led a small church in my home. There was nothing wrong with that. Starting a new church had been the goal from the beginning. But more changed than just where I went to church. I remember attending a conference at the college where I had graduated. As I stood with the crowd to sing worship choruses and then sat to listen to the message, I no longer felt at home. The conference was the same as it had always been, but I was different. Culturally I didn't fit. I belonged in a living room with friends sharing dinner, praying for each other, and discussing Scripture.

I began to feel this way whenever I visited churches, even good churches, even the churches that supported me financially. The traditional church was a nice place to visit. But I no longer wanted to live there. I don't think this is terribly unusual for missionaries. Spending years in a new culture can change a person. Eventually they aren't quite as comfortable in the culture they came from. It is an even bigger issue with missionary kids who are often referred to as "third culture kids" living between the culture their parents left, and the culture they grew up in.

There is nothing inherently good or bad about culture, nor was there anything inherently good or bad about my cultural shift. But the Pharisee in me found a way to make it bad.

I was learning not to label my friends in the poetry community as "the worst of sinners," but I was still not comfortable wearing the label myself. The Pharisee in me needed new sinners to judge. I recognized the command to love my enemies included those who had previously been on the other side of "the culture war," but I now found a new set of enemies to fight.

As soon as I became convicted of my own Pharisaical sins, saw the sinfulness of my pride, and began to recognize how far I was from following in the footsteps of Jesus, I began seeing Pharisees everywhere. I concluded the church was full of them, and wouldn't you know it, they were all worse than me.

I assumed my cultural differences with the traditional church were caused by problems within the church. I would visit a church and judge them because they were not a place where my urban poet friends would be comfortable. Rather than assume this was due to differences in culture, I assumed it was because the church was far from God, refusing to love people the way Jesus loved people.

I had grown up seeing people outside the church as sinners who were far from God; now I began to see people inside the church as sinners who were far from God. In one respect, both beliefs were true. The human race is a collection of sinners, and without the grace of God, we are all far from God.

But there was a problem. I had been a Pharisee who judged people outside of the church based upon externals. God was trying to show me that this was wrong. I had no right to judge people. I was the worst of sinners. But looking at my own sin was uncomfortable. I would rather be the judge than the defendant. So I stopped looking for sin in my own life, and began looking at others in the church.

Go back and look at the poem "What is Christianity?" in chapter 3. Notice how easily I apologize. Then look at how much of my apology is for someone else's sin. Do you see what's going on? It took me years to figure it out.

All the things I listed are evil, and the followers of Christ should be the first to speak out against evil in our churches, and in our world.

But we should begin by confessing the evil in our own lives.

I wasn't really confessing my sin, as much as I was judging other people who had carried the label "Christian" and had not lived up to the example of Christ.

I may be proud, but I've never owned slaves. I may be a Pharisee, but I've never burned a witch or killed an abortion doctor.

I also became good at switching pronouns to let myself off the hook.

"I shouldn't look down on people outside the church," turned into "we shouldn't look down on those outside the church." This was more comfortable. There is safety in numbers. But it wasn't comfortable enough, until finally I looked (down) at the church and said, "You shouldn't look down on those outside the church!"

The Pharisee had returned to the judgment seat, with new defendants to judge.

chapter 24

a church that's irrelevant

Not long after we moved to Chicago, we hosted a short-term missions team from a church in Cedar Rapids, Iowa. It was a more traditional church with a long history. To someone like me who finds it easy to judge based on externals, its best years were behind it. It was small and made up of mostly retired folks. The team did a great job with some community service projects, and they became one of our partnering churches.

A few years later I was invited to speak at the church, so we loaded up our family in the minivan, and braved the ocean of corn that is Iowa.

That weekend changed my view of the traditional church.

From a distance, an untrained eye focused on externals would have been convinced it was either dead or dying. The congregation met in a small brick building. They sat in pews and sang out of hymnbooks with a piano on one side and an organ on the other. The pastor was getting ready to retire, and I wondered if the church would survive his departure.

If they would have asked me, I probably could have given them all kinds of advice on how they could be more relevant and reach out to their community.

But then I got a little closer.

Close enough to see past the log in my eye and notice the people.

I don't remember a lot about the service, but then, I was the speaker. What I do remember was the rest of the day.

There was my visit with Jerry who had been on the mission team to Chicago. Jerry was homebound with numerous health problems, so the pastor and I met him in his home. As we talked it was obvious that he had a prayer life that I could only dream about. And Chicago was a big part of his prayers. He asked about people by name that he had been praying for since his visit to Chicago.

Here was a man whose great physical suffering was nothing compared to the spiritual power he wielded from his knees.

A man whose love and care for people in Chicago he had only met once was so great he was compelled to pray

I was sitting in the presence of greatness.

That evening we were invited to the most amazing bonfire and hayride at a farmhouse in the country. We often say that the church is people, not buildings or programs. I personally believe that the best definition of church is family. These people proved it to me. I don't recall if many of them were related, but I know they were a family. They loved each other, and they loved on my family like nobody's business.

In answering a question during the service my wife had mentioned how proud she was of our daughter who had been saving money for an mp3 player and then gave it away to a ministry that drills wells for villages in Africa. At the bonfire a lady said she happened to have an extra mp3 player she didn't use, and gave it to my daughter.

Here was a church I thought was dead, educating me about love.

I found that when I looked past the specks in my brothers' eyes, I could peer into their hearts.

These hearts were full of love.

Which put my proud heart to shame.

chapter 25

a church that's too relevant

Of course, not every church looks like the little church in Cedar Rapids, some churches show little resemblance with the folks who worship in the little brick building in the middle of Iowa. In Chicago I found one of these churches.

It was a large, multi-site, megachurch, with a well-known pastor and an influence that reached around the globe.

But it was neither big enough, nor influential enough to escape the judgment of an accomplished Pharisee such as myself.

I had judged the little group in Cedar Rapids as dead and irrelevant. When I looked at the megachurch in Chicago, they seemed too relevant. They must have sold out. Surely they had compromised the gospel to appeal to the world.

Looking back I marvel at how I could be so quick to condemn churches across such a broad spectrum of Christendom.

But when a classmate invited my daughter Elizabeth to the youth group at a campus of the megachurch, I was concerned. It wasn't that I thought they weren't Christian, I was just sure they were doing it wrong. As I mentioned earlier, I believed church should be family. I couldn't imagine a family of thousands meeting on multiple campuses. I was certain this made for shallow relationships and a shallow faith. I didn't want Elizabeth to think that this was what church was all about.

I allowed her to go, but first I had a long talk with her about what church really was.

Elizabeth made friends in the youth group, and later on my wife took our daughters to some Sunday services while I was out of town. Our little house church met Friday evenings, so Sundays were open.

They seemed to enjoy it, but I was still not ready. I just couldn't bring myself to attend. But this megachurch seemed to have members everywhere. I couldn't keep from running into them.

Things began to change when they started renting the private school our daughters attended for their monthly men's breakfast. My wife and I were part-time janitors at the school and once a month we had to work around the men's breakfast on Saturday morning. The men were friendly and usually gave us leftovers (which were delicious). My wife encouraged me to attend. A delicious breakfast was more appealing than cleaning classrooms, so I did.

Sitting around a table listening to men discuss their struggle to live godly lives in a difficult world began to change my perspective. These relationships weren't shallow. Their faith ran deep. They had specks in their eyes, but when I stopped focusing on the specks, I found them to be much like me.

By now my wife had gotten me to visit their downtown Chicago campus for a Sunday service. The first time I think she needed to drag me kicking and screaming but going back was much easier.

It wasn't the state of the art audio video equipment or the top of the line worship band that won me over. It was their love for people. From the giant video screen I heard message after message about Christ's love for the "least of these" and His desire for His people to follow in His steps. Whether seeking to address poverty and hunger by sending thousands of seed packets to far away places, or working to improve education by supplying resources to a struggling Chicago public school, their love for God motivated them to love their neighbors. I saw it everywhere I turned.

I don't feel called to a little church in Cedar Rapids, or a megachurch in Chicago, and I'm not naïve enough to think that either church is without problems. But the church is a family, and both of these churches are made up of my brothers and sisters. They have plenty of specks in their eyes. Those specks seem to run in the family.

But when I want to look at specks I try to look in the mirror. I've got a log-sized speck of my own. When I look at my brothers and sisters, I try to see how much they resemble the Father we have in common, and our older brother. . .The Sacrificial Poet.

chapter 26

two kinds of people

I thought this book was finished. In fact, I shifted from writing to editing and even began to focus on publishing. But one thing after another kept holding up the process. I began to get frustrated as the deadlines I had set for myself to finish kept passing.

Then I learned why.

This book is about how God used folks from the poetry scene to educate me, and my education wasn't over.

Over the years at open mics I have routinely heard people talk about issues they were struggling with, and where they went for counseling or therapy. It was assumed that everyone had struggles and needed help. My friends seem to divide the world into two kinds of people.

Those in counseling, and those in denial.

Intellectually I agreed with them. We all have issues. Nobody's perfect. But I'll be honest. I didn't really mean it. I had gone to people for advice, but I had never really undergone counseling. I had issues, but they were small issues. I could handle them myself.

Then I decided to get some training to help other people deal with their issues. Everyone around me seemed to struggle with a multitude of things. I thought it would be good to develop my counseling skills.

I didn't need a counselor. I needed to learn how to be one for everyone else.

Or so I thought.

But my plan to learn how to help others with their issues was interrupted. By my own issues.

Issues I had been denying for way too long.

Night after night of trying unsuccessfully to cry myself to sleep left me with no choice but to acknowledge the truth. I didn't just need help. I needed counseling. I realized my friends were right. There are two types of people, those in counseling and those in denial. After spending my entire life in the second camp, I was ready to humble myself and join the first. I needed help that badly.

The pastor who I had gone to for training became my counselor, helping me process my emotions and reminding me of truths found in Scripture that had been filed away in my head, but never reached my heart.

My heart that was broken.

Just like Molly's.

chapter 27

broken

Little issues can be dealt with internally. You handle them yourself. Sometimes you do business with God. Private business. No one else needs to know.

Bigger issues require a counselor. But they can still be private. Counselors are sworn to secrecy. Your friends can continue to think you have no issues. Molly can go on thinking you're not broken. You have such a good heart.

But real big issues mess with your whole life. They force you to make changes. Changes people notice.

My issues were that big.

They forced changes that affected the way I did my job. There were things I was no longer emotionally able to do. I had to talk to my boss. But talking to my boss wasn't enough. Churches and individuals around the country supported my ministry financially. I had an e-mail list of over 200 people that followed my ministry closely and prayed for me. I knew the changes would lead to questions.

"Why did you make the changes?"

"Is something wrong?"

"Are you okay?"

My issues also affected my relationships within the spoken word community. I wasn't at open mics regularly any more. My friends deserved an explanation.

I had to say something. But what should I say? Issues are usually complicated. Mine were no exception. My counselor told me sharing all the details could do more harm than good.

But I had to say something.

It was easy telling my friends in the spoken word community. It had been several weeks since I had been to open mics, but I went back to let them know what was going on. I didn't give details. I just told them I had to take a break because I had issues. I was broken. I was undergoing counseling. They were very encouraging. They didn't need to know any details. They knew what it was like to be broken. They could identify.

Telling my Christian friends was another matter. I typed up an e-mail to send to my supporters. It didn't give details. It said I had issues. I was broken. I was undergoing counseling. It asked for understanding. It asked for prayer.

I showed it to the leaders at my church before I sent it out. These were godly men I respected. I asked for feedback. They were concerned with how people might respond. They wanted to protect me. They helped me refine it until it was ready. With no small amount of fear I hit "send" and announced my brokenness to my Christian friends.

This left me with questions. Why did the leaders at my church feel the need to protect me from people in my church family? Shouldn't family be the place where broken people can heal? Why was it easier to tell my poetry family?

chapter 28

a tale of two families

There are two kinds of people.

Those in counseling, and those in denial.

Broken people, and people who deny their brokenness.

I didn't have to fear revealing my brokenness to broken people. When broken people hear someone is broken, they don't judge. They identify. Their own brokenness serves as a constant reminder. We live in a broken world. We are hurt by others, and in our honest moments, we know we are guilty of hurting those around us. The Bible calls this sin. Broken people may argue about what to do about it, but they don't deny it is there.

But what about the other group? What about people in denial? You better watch out for them. When they hear someone is broken, judging is a very real option. I know. I lived in that group for most of my life.

Judgment can take many forms. Sometimes it judges people for their brokenness. As if it were their fault. They had made poor choices and now they were paying the price. Sometimes it judges people for not being strong enough to overcome their brokenness. Life isn't fair. What happened may not have been their fault. But why couldn't they suck it up and deal with it? I pulled myself up by my bootstraps. Why don't they?

This was the judgment I feared, and I feared I would find it in the church.

I should be clear. I am not saying that all churches and all Christians are judgmental. To make such a blanket statement would itself be judgmental and wrong. When I told my Christian friends I was going through counseling, I received an overwhelming outpouring of love and support. Some told me stories of their own brokenness and how God was healing them. Others sent encouraging messages and let me know they were praying. I am simply recalling my fear that was shared by the leaders in my church. Some Christians are judgmental and in their judgment they hurt broken people.

To put it another way, some Christians are like me, looking down in judgment on broken people from the lofty pedestals we build.

But the higher the pedestal, the thinner the air and the dizzier one becomes. Until you lose your balance and fall to earth, shatter into pieces and take your place among the broken people.

That's where I found myself, no longer in a position to judge others, but rather fearing judgment.

But also free. Free from the prison that had been my pedestal. Free from the pressure to hide the cracks in my armor and hold it all together. Free to give God my broken pieces and watch the Sacrificial Poet, who is also a Master Artist, put those broken pieces back together.

chapter 29

the Artist

They say the Sacrificial Poet is an Artist
Creator of masterpieces
Exquisite works of beauty
And I thought I believed
Until I entered his showroom

It was anything but beautiful
Piles of shattered pottery
    And broken glass
Blood dripping from the sharp edges of the largest shards
This was no artist's gallery
More likely a crime scene
I wondered
What kind of Artist would create such chaos?
Surely not a good and loving one
Anger and bitterness filled me
What kind of man could bring about such devastation?
He must be mad

But seeing him across the room
My fear evaporated
Far from a raving lunatic
He was calm
Methodically searching through the fragments
With rough hands
Cut and bleeding
Carefully selecting shards of various sizes, shapes, and colors
Piecing together an intricate mosaic
Bringing order from the chaos

My eyes were opened
This was not a showroom
But a studio
He was not the author of destruction and chaos
But a genius bringing beauty from brokenness

The blood
Was His own
The price He paid for picking up the shattered pieces

Then I realized
Beauty can rise from ashes
But only after something burns
And those who close their eyes
And curse the flames
Will never see it

And no Artist's signature piece
Should be judged
Before the Artist cries out
"It is finished!"
And applies
His signature

chapter 30
real church

The view is different from the base of the pedestal. Broken people often see things from the ground that are easily overlooked by those on lofty perches high above it all. The person who has taught me the most about this is Annie. I first met her years ago at an open mic where she read a poem about the old saying, "There are no atheists in foxholes." It included the following lines.

How I want my sense of pride back.
I want to tell my atheist friends
That, like them, I can live just fine
Without God.
But the foxholes they come
One after another
At work
At home
At school
At the shopping mall
At the movies
The foxholes, they are everywhere,
I fall in all the time.
So I fall to my knees
And I ask God
For. . .everything.
Because I,
I have nothing.
Yes, nothing.
I come from dust
And to it I return.

Annie was not an evangelical Christian who tried to write Christian poetry. She was a recovering alcoholic who wrote honest poetry abut her brokenness and her desperate need for God to bring about the healing she was powerless to accomplish on her own.

I was the one who had grown up an evangelical Christian and was trying to write Christian poetry. But I was learning that Christian poetry, even my own Christian poetry, isn't always honest poetry.

Growing up in the church I knew intellectually that I was a fallen sinner with nothing to offer to God. I knew pride was evil and the only way to approach God was in humility. I knew intellectually that I was broken by sin. But some things can't be truly known until they are lived. It wasn't until I experienced brokenness as I tried to cry myself to sleep that I began to truly understand what it is to fall on my face before God and beg for grace and healing.

Annie also taught me about what church should be. She was one of several members of Alcoholics Anonymous I knew in the poetry scene. I was intrigued by their descriptions of meetings where helpless people came together acknowledging their brokenness, admitting they were powerless to achieve healing on their own and were dependant on help from a higher power. It sounded like church. Or at least what church ought to be[17].

Annie told me that in addition to the regular group she attended, she had frequently visited other AA meetings. She said she always felt accepted. She always felt like she belonged. She never feared judgment.

And her experience transcended racial and economic boundaries. It didn't matter how you were dressed or whether you came from a similar background. When you poured a cup of coffee and joined the group you were accepted as family.

One time she accidentally attended a Polish meeting where she didn't know the language and couldn't understand a word they were saying.

But she stayed.

She knew she belonged.

She knew she was among family.

That's what I want from the little church that meets in my home. A place where hopeless, destitute people like me come together and confess they are powerless to heal their own brokenness, but have faith in the Sacrificial Poet who has adopted them into His family and is putting the pieces back together. Bringing beauty from broken fragments.

[17]. I am not suggesting that churches adopt a theology similar to AA which allows members to believe in whatever "higher power" they choose. A church that believes in a higher power other than Jesus Christ would cease to be Christian. But I do think the church can learn from the way AA has become a family for broken people.

A place that accepts hurting, broken people regardless of where they are on their journey, and points them to the Sacrificial Poet who specializes in mosaics.

I came to Chicago to start a church among people far from God. I thought I was bringing them healing. A decade later God is using my experience with those same people to teach me what true church really is and heal my own brokenness.

Only the Sacrificial Poet could write such a beautiful poem.

chapter 31
choose your chapter

Living between two worlds also makes it difficult to write a book. A book that is written for the Christian market may not communicate clearly to the spoken word community, and vice versa. This has been an incredible challenge, and a cause of continued editing and revisions. Hopefully to this point I have communicated in a way that both groups can understand.

But there are things I need to say that are directed more specifically at one group or the other. I struggled with how to do this, until I was reminded of my childhood library.

Growing up I enjoyed reading "Choose Your Own Adventure" books. Today occasionally I see my daughters reading them. The beauty of a "Choose Your Own Adventure" book is the reader controls the story. At the end of each chapter is a choice.

> *If you want to trust the aliens and go aboard their spaceship, turn to page X. If you want to retreat to a defensible position and prepare to fight them, turn to page Y*

So here is your chance to choose your own adventure. If you are part of the Christian subculture turn to page 105 and read chapter 32. If you are not part of the Christian subculture turn to page 109 and read chapter 32.

chapter 32

for my christian family

I've read many Christian books. I think I know what sells. When it comes to missions, we want to hear stories about pioneers taking the gospel to evil, dark places. We want to hear about someone preaching to a tribe of cannibals. We like missionaries who "convert" the worst of sinners. Missionaries who pull this off become evangelical celebrities. They write best selling books and are in high demand to speak at churches and conferences.

Before I moved to Chicago, that was my goal, to go where no Christian had gone before, shine the light in the darkness, and take the truth to people who were terribly wicked and far from God.

Looking back it seems ridiculous, but I assumed that any book that resulted would have been about how God had used me to bring about transformation in the lives of the sinful broken people I would encounter.

That's a formula for a best selling book.

Of course, it's also a great way to alienate my poet friends. Just as no one wants to be a conversion project, no one wants to be cast in such a negative light; especially by someone they consider a friend.

There is one other reason I can't write such a book. It wouldn't be true. My friends in the poetry community are not the worst of sinners and I suspect many, like Maggot, are not far from God. Not to mention the fact that I haven't converted them. There has been no "Great Awakening" in Chicago's spoken word community. God hasn't used me to transform Chicago, but He has used Chicago to transform me. He has done this by showing me the log in my eye. The more I work to remove it, the less qualified I feel to judge. The more I have gotten to know people the more I doubt my original judgments.

He has shown me my brokenness and that I am powerless to heal without Him. I am no longer trying to reach down from my lofty pedestal to help the broken people below.

So I can't impress you by writing a book about how I'm a beacon of light shining in the darkest places where everyone is far from God.

That would be a lie, and would alienate my friends in the spoken word community who know better.

Instead of writing about taking the good news to the worst of sinners, I am writing about how I found out I was the worst of sinners. This may not make me a missionary celebrity, but at least it's honest.

And I'm trying to be more honest.

My job is not to find the worst of sinners and transform them. My job is to recognize I am the worst of sinners and let the Sacrificial Poet transform me.

My job is not to attack the speck in my brother's eye. My job is to let the Sacrificial Poet remove the log from my eye. Only then can I see my brother through His eyes. Eyes that see past the specks to the image of God that dwells within.

I need to stop wearing a mask to convince them I have a good heart, and let them see the Sacrificial Poet, who is the Great Physician healing my own broken sinful heart.

I need Jesus today as much as anyone.

And I need to learn to love others the way Jesus loves them, without judging how far they are from God.

I am writing this book in hopes that my Christian brothers can learn from my mistakes. Maybe then they can keep whatever specks they have in their eyes from growing into a log like mine did.

Don't use externals to judge people as far from God or unlikely to follow Jesus. The Sacrificial Poet sometimes shows up in the least likely of places. The world is full of people who are closer to God than we will ever know. They don't need Christians who have their act together to make conversion projects out of them and fix them. They need Christians like Paul who recognize their own sin and are experiencing the unlimited patience and mercy of the Sacrificial Poet.

If you do judge people, don't compound the error by throwing stones.

Don't hide behind a mask on top of a pedestal and try to impress people with your judgment and stone-throwing accuracy. Convincing people you are righteous doesn't make it so.

I know. I speak from experience.

Which is why I need to apologize. Many of you have been the victims of my judging, and some have felt the sting of stones hurled in your direction. Forgive me for focusing on the specks I perceive in your eyes rather than the log in my own.

The Sacrificial Poet has been working on that log, but He has yet to totally remove it. Sometimes it still clouds my vision.

I hope you will join me in the conversation, and may we both grow closer to the Sacrificial Poet, as we drop our stones and let Him wipe the specks (and logs) from our eyes. Until the day He finally leads us home, where He puts all our broken pieces together creating a masterpiece of His Glory.

Now turn to page 111 for chapter 33.

chapter 32

for my poetry family

I am a follower of Jesus, albeit an imperfect one. I've tried to hide my imperfections for too long. But I'm learning that it is in my imperfection that I meet Him. He can only heal me where I am broken. His strength reaches down to lift the burdens that threaten to crush my weak shoulders.

So to my friends in the poetry community, please don't use my flaws (or any other Christian's flaws) as an excuse to stop looking for the truth. Rather, realize that my flaws are evidence of how much I need Jesus.

I'm sorry for all the years I judged you based upon externals, and was all too willing to throw stones in judgment. Forgive me for those stones, and for the masks I've worn to convince people I'm qualified to throw them.

Thank you for teaching me so much about myself. I owe you an incredible debt for years of sharing your lives with me. Our late night conversations have taught me more about my faith than seminary ever did. My search for answers to your tough questions has driven me to continually dig for truth. The answers I have found may not have converted you, but they have helped me understand my own conversion.

God used you to preach the gospel to me, showing me the log in my eye, and that in my brokenness I am unable to remove it without Him.

God used you to show me that I need to honestly face my own brokenness and deal with my own sin rather than judge others.

For this, I thank you.

I don't consider you conversion projects. You are the unexpected friends in the most unexpected places that God is using to enrich my life. Thank you.

I pray that our conversations continue, our friendship grows, and somehow I can help you on your journey as much as you have helped me. My prayer is that one-day we all arrive safely home where the Divine Poet is waiting with open arms.

chapter 33

waiting for adam

I was desperate
I was empty like Eden
Waiting for Adam
Weeping like Rachel
For My children
Because they were no more

In the garden they rejected Me
So with a heavy heart
I watched them leave
to wander
With a promise
that one day
I would make a Way
home

And I waited
But not idly

I held the universe in place
Kept the earth in orbit
Sent rain to water the fields
And snow to cover the mountains
But it wasn't enough

I reached out
Sent visions and dreams
Prophets and Poets
But it wasn't enough

I spoke through a burning bush
And the mouth of a donkey
My voice thundered from a mountain peak
and whispered on the wind
But it wasn't enough

I appeared as a Pillar of Cloud by day
And Fire by night

But it wasn't enough

I wrote on stone tablets
And the plaster wall of a palace
But it wasn't enough

I sent water from a rock
Fed them bread from heaven
Flocks of quail as far as the eye could see
But it wasn't enough

I split the sea
Made a path through the river
But it wasn't enough

The sun stood still
Fire from heaven consumed a flooded altar
But it wasn't enough

I closed the mouths of lions
I opened barren wombs
But it wasn't enough

I quenched the fury of flames
But it wasn't enough

I protected my prophets
In an ark of wood
A basket of reeds
And the belly of a whale
But it wasn't enough

I cured lepers
I raised the dead to life
But it wasn't enough

Then in the fullness of time
I sent them My Son
Seed of Abraham
Child of the Promise
He healed the sick
Gave sight to the blind
Showed them The Way of Love
The Way home
But it wasn't enough

They killed him

And they continued to wander

But His death was just the beginning
For The Way of Love is never a dead end
And when He rose, it signaled death's end

It was finally
Enough

But I am still waiting for Adam
Still waiting for fellowship
With his progeny
Scattered across the globe

I am still waiting for Adam
And a new Eden
Restored by My hand
And inhabited by My Children
When they finally find
The Way home

epilogue
why I believe

[11] When I was a child, I talked like a child, I thought like a child, I reasoned like a child. When I became a man, I put childish ways behind me. [12] Now we see but a poor reflection as in a mirror: then we shall see face to face, Now I know in part; then I shall know fully, even as I am fully known. [18]

I wasn't born believing
I was brainwashed as a child
I accepted everything I was taught
But acceptance isn't belief
As a child I spouted answers to questions I had never asked
But answers without questions
Are not answers
Just clichés

As a young man
The questions came
And I found that my answers were
Not always satisfying
They were simple, childish attempts
To understand a universe
Full of infinite paradoxes
They weren't exactly wrong
But they were at best incomplete
I wanted more
    The missing puzzle pieces
        The mystery unlocked

As I grew older
I realized my answers weren't the only thing lacking
I was lacking
I couldn't handle the real answers
The real answers are infinite

[18.] 1 Corinthians 13:11–12

The more I tried to cram them in my finite head
The more it hurt
I began to fear it would burst
Before I even began to understand

At this realization
I lost hope of ever finding all the answers
And I learned what faith was

So why do I believe?

Not because I have all the answers
But because there are too many questions
And without belief
I have no answers

Why do I believe in God?

Not because believers are such wonderful people
Frankly, they suck
No, I believe in God because I suck
I need a God who loves sucky people
When I look at believers
I'm convinced He must

What do I believe about God?
I believe what I believe about God matters
But not nearly as much
As what God believes about me
Only one of us is ever wrong
And that would be me

I believe I didn't choose God
God chose me
For some impossible to understand reason
God loved a sucky person
With no answers
I call it Grace
I don't understand it
But I believe

the prequel

The Sacrificial Poet
act 1

The heavens declare the glory of God;
*   the skies proclaim the work of his hands.*
Day after day they pour fourth speech;
*   night after night they display knowledge.*
There is no speech or language
*   where their voice is not heard.*
Their voice goes out into all the earth,
*   their words to the ends of the world[19].*

In the beginning was the Word
And the Word spoke. . . .
*   Poetry*
Breathing life
Into an epic masterpiece
Revealing His heart
He saw it and it was good

At the pinnacle of His masterpiece was man
Made in His image
With the task of preserving the poem
*   Memorizing it word for word*
*   Reciting it aloud so that all may hear the heart of its Creator*
*   Revealed in His verse*

But man failed
Far from preserving and protecting
He perverted and polluted
It still revealed the glorious Heart of its Creator
But now that revelation was marred
The glory often hidden by wickedness

The Eternal Word spoke again
Cursing His Poem
*   And the man who had defaced it*
Promising restoration
No matter the cost

[19]. Psalm 19:1–4

act 2

The Word became flesh
Written into His masterpiece
The Sacrificial Poet
Spoke a new poem
Redeeming His creation

The Word was grieved
His masterpiece lost
He wept over it
  Beautiful still
    yet marred and distorted
  The heavens declaring His glory
    as they groaned in frustration
  The skies proclaiming the work of His hands
    while suffering in bondage to decay

But He loved it still
With a love willing to pay any price
So the Word became flesh
The Perfect Poet wrote Himself into His poem
Revealing His Perfect Heart in a way no mere work of poetry
  could
He walked among us as a Healer
  restoring the damage
    bringing beauty from ashes
His words were parables
His life was poetry
He called out to all who would listen
                    "Follow Me!"

But we rejected Him
We who had brought death and decay to His creation
  now plotted to kill its Creator
In the greatest act of vandalism
The Light of the World
  was darkened
The Eternal Word
  was silenced

The Life that was the Light of men
   died in the dark at the hands of men.
The One who had breathed life into the dust of the ground
   Breathed His last and was buried in the ground

Perfection had once again been defeated

Or so it would seem

But this was the plan

The Sacrificial Poet was born
   to stand before the Judge
     be the sacrifice
       overcome the devastation

The only way to end suffering, death and decay
   was for the Sacrificial Poet to bear it away

Carry it to the grave

And leave it there

When He rose the Light began to shine again
The Eternal Word spoke again
And the Sacrificial Poet uttered a poem
   Greater than His original masterpiece
A poem revealing not only His great power and glory
   But His grace and mercy
A poem revealing His heart of love
   Like never before
A poem outlasting the heavens and the earth
A poem that never changes
     but is new every morning
A love poem that will take eternity to read
   But be summed up in two words.
                  "Follow Me!"

act 3

"Follow Me!"
Speak My Words
Learn My Poetry
Live My Poetry
Love

The Sacrificial Poet still speaks
He who powerfully spoke the universe into existence
  today speaks with greater power
Many have tried to harness this power
  building kingdoms and empires in His name
But the kingdoms they build are not His kingdom
For His kingdom is not of this world
His kingdom invades this world with a strength hidden in weakness
The Lion became a Lamb to lead a flock of sheep
These sheep hear His voice and follow Him
He engraves His poetry on their hearts
Transforming them
Until they love with His Love
Echoing His poetry

Poetry not merely written
  but lived

Poetry of
  asking
    seeking
      and knocking

  of brokenness being restored,
    weakness being transformed into strength
      fools searching out Wisdom
        and love that casts out fear

  of forgiveness and sacrifice

Poetry that says "Follow me, as I follow Him!"

Made in the USA
Charleston, SC
19 March 2014